Sophocles'

Antigone
In Plain and Simple English

BookCaps™ Study Guides

www.SwipeBook.com

Table of Contents

Characters

ANTIGONE and **ISMENE** - daughters of Oedipus and sisters of Polyneices

and Eteocles.

CREON, King of Thebes.

HAEMON, Son of Creon, betrothed to Antigone.

EURYDICE, wife of Creon.

TEIRESIAS, the prophet.

CHORUS, of Theban elders.

A WATCHMAN

A MESSENGER

A SECOND MESSENGER

ANTIGONE and **ISMENE** before the Palace gates.

Argument

Antigone, daughter of Oedipus, the late king of Thebes, in defiance of Creon who rules in his stead, resolves to bury her brother Polyneices, slain in his attack on Thebes. She is caught in the act by Creon's watchmen and brought before the king. She justifies her action, asserting that she was bound to obey the eternal laws of right and wrong in spite of any human ordinance. Creon, unrelenting, condemns her to be immured in a rock-hewn chamber. His son Haemon, to whom Antigone is betrothed, pleads in vain for her life and threatens to die with her. Warned by the seer Teiresias Creon repents him and hurries to release Antigone from her rocky prison. But he is too late: he finds lying side by side Antigone who had hanged herself and Haemon who also has perished by his own hand. Returning to the palace he sees within the dead body of his queen who on learning of her son's death has stabbed herself to the heart.

Antigone, daughter of Oedipus, the dead King of Thebes, resolves to bury her brother Polyneices, killed in his attack on Thebes. This defies the order of Creon, who now rules Thebes. She is caught in the act and brought before the king. She justifies her action by saying that she must follow the laws of Heaven despite what any man might say. Creon, unmoved, orders that she should be walled up in a cave. His son Haemon, Antigone's fiancé, pleads in vain for her life and threatens to die with her. Warned by the prophet Teiresias Creon repents and rushes to release Antigone. But he is too late: he finds Antigone dead from suicide and Haemon kills himself in front of Creon. Returning to the palace he sees within the dead body of his queen, who stabbed herself through the heart when she heard of her son's death.

ANTIGONE

Ismene, sister of my blood and heart,

See'st thou how Zeus would in our lives fulfill

The weird of Oedipus, a world of woes!

For what of pain, affliction, outrage, shame,

Is lacking in our fortunes, thine and mine?

And now this proclamation of today

Made by our Captain-General to the State,

What can its purport be? Didst hear and heed,

Or art thou deaf when friends are banned as foes?

Ismene, sister of my blood and heart,

Do you see how Zeus wants to make us suffer

The curse of Oedipus, a world of sorrow!

For what pain, affliction, outrage, shame,

Is missing from our fortunes, yours and mine?

And now today's proclamation,

Made by our leader to the State,

What is its purpose? Did you hear and note it,

Or are you deaf when friends are exiled as enemies?

ISMENE

To me, Antigone, no word of friends

Has come, or glad or grievous, since we twain

Were reft of our two brethren in one day

By double fratricide; and since i' the night

Our Argive leaguers fled, no later news

Has reached me, to inspirit or deject.

To me, Antigone, I haven't had any word of friends,

Good or bad, since we two

Were stripped of our two brothers in one day

When they killed each other; and since the night

The besiegers from Argos fled, I have had

No further news, saddening or cheering.

ANTIGONE

I know 'twas so, and therefore summoned thee

Beyond the gates to breathe it in thine ear.

I knew this was the case, and so I called you

Outside the gates to whisper it to you.

ISMENE

What is it? Some dark secret stirs thy breast.

What is it? You have some dark secret.

ANTIGONE

What but the thought of our two brothers dead,

What could it be but the thought of our two dead brothers,

The one by Creon graced with funeral rites,

One given a proper funeral by Creon,

The other disappointed? Eteocles

The other denied one? Eteocles

He hath consigned to earth (as fame reports)

Was put in the ground (so it's said)

With obsequies that use and wont ordain,

With all the customary fitting ceremonies,

So gracing him among the dead below.

So that he would go properly to the underworld.

But Polyneices, a dishonored corse,

But Polynieces, a dishonored corpse

(So by report the royal edict runs)

Cannot be buried, no-one can grieve for him

No man may bury him or make lament--

(This is what I hear the royal order is);

Must leave him tombless and unwept, a feast

He must be left without a tomb, without mourners,

For kites to scent afar and swoop upon.

A feast for the kites to smell from far off and swoop upon.

Such is the edict (if report speak true)

This is the ruling (if the reports are true)

Of Creon, our most noble Creon, aimed

Of Creon, our most noble Creon, aimed

At thee and me, aye me too; and anon

At you and me, yes, me as well; and shortly

He will be here to promulgate, for such

He'll be here to spread, for those

As have not heard, his mandate; 'tis in sooth

Who haven't heard it, his orders;

No passing humor, for the edict says

It's obviously not something

He's taking lightly, as the order says

Whoe'er transgresses shall be stoned to death.

That anyone who disobeys will be stoned to death.

So stands it with us; now 'tis thine to show

That's the situation; now it's up to you to show

If thou art worthy of thy blood or base.

If you live up to your heritage or not.

ISMENE

But how, my rash, fond sister, in such case

But how, my hasty, dear sister, in this case,

Can I do anything to make or mar?

Can I do anything, good or bad?

ANTIGONE

Say, wilt thou aid me and abet? Decide.

Tell me if you'll help and support me. Decide.

ISMENE

In what bold venture? What is in thy thought?

In what daring venture? What are you thinking of?

ANTIGONE

Lend me a hand to bear the corpse away.

Help me carry off the corpse.

ISMENE

What, bury him despite the interdict?

What, bury him in spite of the order?

ANTIGONE

My brother, and, though thou deny him, thine

My brother, and though you won't recognize him yours too.

No man shall say that I betrayed a brother.

No man shall say that I betrayed a brother.

ISMENE

Wilt thou persist, though Creon has forbid?

Will you go through with this, though Creon forbids it?

ANTIGONE

What right has he to keep me from my own?

What right has he to keep me from my own family?

ISMENE

Bethink thee, sister, of our father's fate,

Abhorred, dishonored, self-convicted of sin,

Blinded, himself his executioner.

Think of his mother-wife (ill sorted names)

Think, sister, what happened to our father,

Hated, dishonored, convicted of sin by himself,

Blinded, his own executioner.

Think of his mother-wife (names which should not go together),

Done by a noose herself had twined to death

And last, our hapless brethren in one day,

Both in a mutual destiny involved,

Self-slaughtered, both the slayer and the slain.

Bethink thee, sister, we are left alone;

Shall we not perish wretchedest of all,

If in defiance of the law we cross

A monarch's will?--weak women, think of that,

Not framed by nature to contend with men.

Remember this too that the stronger rules;

We must obey his orders, these or worse.

Therefore I plead compulsion and entreat

Killed with a noose she knotted herself,

And lastly, our unlucky brothers, who on the same day,

Caught up in a shared fate,

Killed themselves, each one killer and victim.

Think, sister, we are left alone;

Will we not die the most wretched death of all,

If against the law we ignore

A monarch's orders? – we are weak women, remember,

Not built by nature to fight with men.

Remember this too, that the stonger one rules;

We must obey his orders, these or even worse ones.

So I say that I am forced not to do this and ask

The dead to pardon. I perforce obey

The powers that be. 'Tis foolishness, I ween,

To overstep in aught the golden mean.

The dead to forgive me. I have to obey

The ruling powers. It's stupidity, I think,

To try and rebel against the king in anything.

ANTIGONE

I urge no more; nay, wert thou willing still,

I won't try to persuade you; in fact, if you now said you would,

I would not welcome such a fellowship.

I wouldn't want you with me.

Go thine own way; myself will bury him.

Go your own way, I shall bury him alone.

How sweet to die in such employ, to rest,--

How sweet to die doing such a task, to rest –

Sister and brother linked in love's embrace--

A brother and sister linked in a loving hug –

A sinless sinner, banned awhile on earth,

A sinless sinner, condemned a while on earth

But by the dead commended; and with them

But applauded by the dead; and I shall live

I shall abide for ever. As for thee,

With them forever. As for you,

Scorn, if thou wilt, the eternal laws of Heaven.

Reject the eternal laws of Heaven if you want.

ISMENE

I scorn them not, but to defy the State

Or break her ordinance I have no skill.

I do not reject them, but I haven't the skill

To stand up to the State or break her laws.

ANTIGONE

A specious pretext. I will go alone

To lay my dearest brother in the grave.

A poor excuse. I will go alone

To place my dearest brother in his grave.

ISMENE

My poor, fond sister, how I fear for thee!

My poor, dear sister, how I fear for you!

ANTIGONE

O waste no fears on me; look to thyself.

Don't be frightened for me; have a look at yourself.

ISMENE

At least let no man know of thine intent,

But keep it close and secret, as will I.

At least don't tell anyone what you're up to,

Keep it secret and hidden, as I will.

ANTIGONE

O tell it, sister; I shall hate thee more

If thou proclaim it not to all the town.

Oh, tell everyone, sister; I'll hate you more

If you don't tell the whole town.

ISMENE

Thou hast a fiery soul for numbing work.

You have a brave soul for such dangerous work.

ANTIGONE

I pleasure those whom I would liefest please.

I give pleasure to those I would most like to please.

ISMENE

If thou succeed; but thou art doomed to fail.

If you succeed; but you're doomed to fail.

ANTIGONE

When strength shall fail me, yes, but not before.

If my strength fails then so will I, but not before that.

ISMENE

But, if the venture's hopeless, why essay?

But why try it, when the thing's impossible?

ANTIGONE

Sister, forbear, or I shall hate thee soon,

And the dead man will hate thee too, with cause.

Say I am mad and give my madness rein

To wreck itself; the worst that can befall

Is but to die an honorable death.

Sister, give up, or I shall soon hate you,

And the dead man shall hate you too, justifiably.

Call me mad and leave my madness free

To destroy itself; the worst that can happen

Is that I'll die an honorable death.

ISMENE

Have thine own way then; 'tis a mad endeavor,

Yet to thy lovers thou art dear as ever.

Have it your own way; it's a mad plan,

But those who love you love you just as much.

[Exeunt]

CHORUS

(Str. 1)

Sunbeam, of all that ever dawn upon

Our seven-gated Thebes the brightest ray,

O eye of golden day,

How fair thy light o'er Dirce's fountain shone,

Speeding upon their headlong homeward course,

Far quicker than they came, the Argive force;

Putting to flight the argent shields,

The host with scutcheons white.

Against our land the proud invader came

To vindicate fell Polyneices' claim.

Like to an eagle swooping low,

On pinions white as new fall'n snow.

With clanging scream, a horsetail plume his crest,

The aspiring lord of Argos onward pressed.

Sunbeam, you are the brightest that ever

Dawned on our seven gated Thebes,

Oh golden eye of day,

How lovely your light shone over Dirce's fountain,

Sending on their hurtling homeward way,

Far quicker than they came, the army of Argos;

Putting to flight the silver shields,

The army with their white decorations.

Against our land the proud invader came

To pursue evil Polyneice's claim,

Like an eagle swooping down

With his snow-white claws.

With a clanging din and a horsetail plume in his helmet,

The hopeful lord of Argos pressed onwards.

(Ant.1)

Hovering around our city walls he waits,

His spearmen raven at our seven gates.

But ere a torch our crown of towers could burn,

Ere they had tasted o'er our blood, they turn

Forced by the Dragon; in their rear

The din of Ares panic-struck they hear.

For Zeus who hates the braggart's boast

Beheld that gold-bespangled host;

As at the goal the paean they upraise,

He waited, besieging our city walls,

His hungry spearmen at our seven gates,

But before a torch could burn our towers,

Before they'd tasted our blood, they turned,

Forced by the Dragon; in their rear

They heard with panic the noise of war.

For Zeus, who hates arrogance,

Saw that gold covered army;

And as they raised a shout of triumph at reaching their

goal

He struck them with his forked lightning blaze.

He struck them with his forked lightning.

(Str. 2)

To earthy from earth rebounding, down he crashed;

He smashed down upon the earth,

The fire-brand from his impious hand was dashed,

The firebrand was snatched from the blasphemous hand,

As like a Bacchic reveler on he came,

As he staggered on like a drunk at an orgy,

Outbreathing hate and flame,

Breathing hate and flame,

And tottered. Elsewhere in the field,

And fell. Elsewhere in the battle

Here, there, great Area like a war-horse wheeled;

Here, there, great Mars wheeled like a war horse,

Beneath his car down thrust

Spearing out from his chariot,

Our foemen bit the dust.

And our enemies bit the dust.

Seven captains at our seven gates

Seven captains hammered on

Thundered; for each a champion waits,

Our seven gates; there was an opponent for each,

Each left behind his armor bright,

And each left behind his bright armor,

Trophy for Zeus who turns the fight;

A trophy for Zeus who turned the tide;

Save two alone, that ill-starred pair

There were just two who remain, that unfortunate pair,

One mother to one father bare,

Born of the same parents,

Who lance in rest, one 'gainst the other

Who charged with their lances, one against the other,

Drave, and both perished, brother slain by brother.

Drove them home and both died, brother killed by brother.

(Ant. 2)

Now Victory to Thebes returns again

Now Victory comes back to Thebes,

And smiles upon her chariot-circled plain.

And smiles on her plain, circled with chariots.

Now let feast and festal should

Now let feast and festival

Memories of war blot out.

Blot out the memories of war.

Let us to the temples throng,

Dance and sing the live night long.

god of Thebes, lead thou the round.

Bacchus, shaker of the ground!

Let us end our revels here;

Lo! Creon our new lord draws near,

Crowned by this strange chance, our king.

What, I marvel, pondering?

Why this summons? Wherefore call

Us, his elders, one and all,

Bidding us with him debate,

On some grave concern of State?

Let us all go to the temples

And dance and sing the whole night through.

god of Thebes, lead the song,

Bacchus, the ground shaker!

Now let's stop our celebrations;

Look! Creon, our new lord, is coming,

Crowned, by the twists of fate, our king.

What, I wonder, is he thinking of?

Why has he summoned us? Why has he called

All of the elders,

Calling us to debate with him

Some important affairs of State?

[Enter **CREON**]

CREON

Elders, the gods have righted once again

Our storm-tossed ship of state, now safe in port.

But you by special summons I convened

As my most trusted councilors; first, because

I knew you loyal to Laius of old;

Again, when Oedipus restored our State,

Both while he ruled and when his rule was o'er,

Ye still were constant to the royal line.

Now that his two sons perished in one day,

Brother by brother murderously slain,

Elders, the gods have steadied

Our storm-tossed ship of state, now safely in port.

But I have gathered you by special summons

As my most trusted advisers; firstly, because

I know that you were loyal to Laius in the old days,

And then as you were also loyal to Oedipus when he saved our state,

Both when he ruled and when his rule was finished,

You stayed loyal to the royal family.

Now that his two sons have died in one day,

Brother murdered by brother,

By right of kinship to the Princes dead,

I claim and hold the throne and sovereignty.

Yet 'tis no easy matter to discern

The temper of a man, his mind and will,

Till he be proved by exercise of power;

And in my case, if one who reigns supreme

Swerve from the highest policy, tongue-tied

By fear of consequence, that man I hold,

And ever held, the basest of the base.

And I contemn the man who sets his friend

Before his country. For myself, I call

To witness Zeus, whose eyes are everywhere,

If I perceive some mischievous design

To sap the State, I will not hold my tongue;

Nor would I reckon as my private friend

A public foe, well knowing that the State

Is the good ship that holds our fortunes all:

Farewell to friendship, if she suffers wreck.

Such is the policy by which I seek

To serve the Commons and conformably

I have proclaimed an edict as concerns

The sons of Oedipus; Eteocles

Who in his country's battle fought and fell,

The foremost champion--duly bury him

With all observances and ceremonies

That are the guerdon of the heroic dead.

But for the miscreant exile who returned

Minded in flames and ashes to blot out

I claim and hold the throne and kingship,

By right of my relation to the dead princes.

But it isn't easy to tell

The strength of a man, of his mind and willpower,

Until it is tested once he's in power;

And for me, if anyone who has the highest power

Dodges following the best policy, not speaking

For fear of the consequences, I have always

Thought that man the lowest of the low.

And I despise the man who puts his friend

Before his country. For myself,

I swear by Zeus, who sees all,

That if I uncover some cunning plan

To damage the State, I will not be silent;

Nor would I have a public enemy

As a private friend, knowing that the State

Is the good ship that carries all our futures:

Friendship will be ended if she is wrecked.

This is my policy as I try

To serve the people, and so

I have issued an order in relation

To the sons of Oedipus: Eteocles,

Who fought and died for his country

As a hero – he should be buried

With all the respect and ceremony

That are the right of the honored dead.

But for that wretched exile who returned,

Meaning with flames to destroy

His father's city and his father's gods,

And glut his vengeance with his kinsmen's blood,

Or drag them captive at his chariot wheels--

For Polyneices 'tis ordained that none

Shall give him burial or make mourn for him,

But leave his corpse unburied, to be meat

For dogs and carrion crows, a ghastly sight.

So am I purposed; never by my will

Shall miscreants take precedence of true men,

But all good patriots, alive or dead,

Shall be by me preferred and honored.

His father's city and his father's gods,

And satisfy his thirst for revenge with the blood of his kinsmen,

Or to drag them as prisoners behind his chariot –

For Polynieces I rule that nobody

Shall give him a burial or mourn for him,

But that his corpse should be left unburied as meat

For the dogs and carrion crows, a horrid sight.

This is my decision; never will I let

Scoundrels be honored over true men,

But all good patriots, alive or dead,

Shall be promoted and honored by me.

CHORUS

Son of Menoeceus, thus thou will'st to deal

With him who loathed and him who loved our State.

Thy word is law; thou canst dispose of us

The living, as thou will'st, as of the dead.

Son of Menoeceus, that's your choice of how you deal

With the one who loved and the one who loathed our State.

Your word is law; you can do with us,

The living, as you wish, just as you can with the dead.

CREON

See then ye execute what I ordain.

Then see you do as I have ordered.

CHORUS

On younger shoulders lay this grievous charge.

This task should be given to younger men.

CREON

Fear not, I've posted guards to watch the corpse.

Don't worry, I have sent guards to watch the corpse.

CHORUS

What further duty would'st thou lay on us?

What else do you want us to do?

CREON

Not to connive at disobedience.

Not to allow disobedience.

CHORUS

No man is mad enough to court his death.

No man would be so stupid as to risk his death.

CREON

The penalty is death: yet hope of gain

Hath lured men to their ruin oftentimes.

The penalty is death, but the hope of profit

Has often led men to their downfall.

[Enter GUARD]

GUARD

My lord, I will not make pretense to pant

And puff as some light-footed messenger.

My lord, I will not pretend to puff and pant

As if I'd just run all the way here.

In sooth my soul beneath its pack of thought

Made many a halt and turned and turned again;

For conscience plied her spur and curb by turns.

"Why hurry headlong to thy fate, poor fool?"

She whispered. Then again, "If Creon learn

This from another, thou wilt rue it worse."

Thus leisurely I hastened on my road;

Much thought extends a furlong to a league.

But in the end the forward voice prevailed,

To face thee. I will speak though I say nothing.

For plucking courage from despair methought,

'Let the worst hap, thou canst but meet thy fate.'

Truly, my soul, under its burden of thoughts,

Often stopped, turned back, turned round again;

My conscience drove me on and pulled me back in turn.

"Why are you rushing headlong to your fate, poor fool?"

She whispered. The she said, "If Creon learns

About this from someone else, it'll be even worse for you."

So I went along my way, sometimes quick, sometimes slow;

Thinking makes short distances long ones.

But in the end the voice saying go forward won.

So I came to face you. I will speak even if I say nothing,

For taking courage in my despair I thought,

"Let the worst happen, all you can do is face your fate."

CREON

What is thy news? Why this despondency?

What's the news? Why this despair?

GUARD

Let me premise a word about myself?

I neither did the deed nor saw it done,

Nor were it just that I should come to harm.

Can I say a word about my position?

I didn't do the deed or see it done,

And it wouldn't be fair for me to be punished.

CREON

Thou art good at parry, and canst fence about

Some matter of grave import, as is plain.

You're a good swordsman, you can fence around

What is obviously an important matter.

GUARD

The bearer of dread tidings needs must quake.

The bearer of bad news should be afraid.

CREON

Then, sirrah, shoot thy bolt and get thee gone.

Then, sir, say your piece and go.

GUARD

Well, it must out; the corpse is buried; someone

E'en now besprinkled it with thirsty dust,

Performed the proper ritual--and was gone.

Well, it has to be said; the corpse is buried. Someone

Just now covered it with the dry earth,

Performed the proper ceremony and was gone.

CREON

What say'st thou? Who hath dared to do this thing?

What are you saying? Who dared to do this?

GUARD

I cannot tell, for there was ne'er a trace

Of pick or mattock--hard unbroken ground,

Without a scratch or rut of chariot wheels,

No sign that human hands had been at work.

When the first sentry of the morning watch

I can't tell, for there were no marks

Of a pickaxe or hoe – hard unbroken ground,

Without a scratch or rut from chariot wheels,

No sign that human hands had been at work.

When the first sentry of the morning shift

Gave the alarm, we all were terror-stricken.

The corpse had vanished, not interred in earth,

But strewn with dust, as if by one who sought

To avert the curse that haunts the unburied dead:

Of hound or ravening jackal, not a sign.

Thereat arose an angry war of words;

Guard railed at guard and blows were like to end it,

For none was there to part us, each in turn

Suspected, but the guilt brought home to none,

From lack of evidence. We challenged each

The ordeal, or to handle red-hot iron,

Or pass through fire, affirming on our oath

Our innocence--we neither did the deed

Ourselves, nor know who did or compassed it.

Our quest was at a standstill, when one spake

And bowed us all to earth like quivering reeds,

For there was no gainsaying him nor way

To escape perdition: Ye_are_bound_to_tell

The_King,_ye_cannot_hide_it; so he spake.

And he convinced us all; so lots were cast,

And I, unlucky scapegoat, drew the prize.

So here I am unwilling and withal

Unwelcome; no man cares to hear ill news.

Gave the alarm, we were all terrified.

The corpse had vanished, not buried in the earth

But covered with dust, as if someone was trying

To ward off the curse that falls on the unburied dead;

There was no sign of dogs or hungry jackals.

Then a great argument started;

Guards shouted at each other and it seemed a fight would follow,

For there was no-one to act as peacemaker;

Each one of us was suspected, but nobody could be proved guilty,

For there was no evidence. We challenged each one

To be tortured, or handle red hot iron,

Or walk through the fire, swearing our innocence

On oath – we neither did this thing

Ourselves, nor did we know who did or planned it.

Our investigation ground to a halt, when one spoke

Who made us all bow down like quivering reeds,

For there was no denying what he said nor any way

To escape his sentence: "You must tell

The King, you cannot hide it." That's what he said,

And he convinced us he was right; we drew lots,

And I, unlucky victim, drew the short straw.

So here I am, unwilling and also

Unwelcome, as no man wants to hear bad news.

CHORUS

I had misgivings from the first, my liege,

Of something more than natural at work.

I thought from the start, your highness,

That there was something more than natural going on.

CREON

O cease, you vex me with your babblement;

Oh be quiet, your babbling annoys me;

I am like to think you dote in your old age.

It looks like you're going soft in your old age.

Is it not arrant folly to pretend

Don't you think it's ridiculous to suppose

That gods would have a thought for this dead man?

The gods would care anything for this dead man?

Did they forsooth award him special grace,

Did they show him special favors,

And as some benefactor bury him,

And bury him like a good man,

Who came to fire their hallowed sanctuaries,

The man who came to burn their holy sanctuaries,

To sack their shrines, to desolate their land,

To destroy their shrines, lay waste to their land

And scout their ordinances? Or perchance

And break their laws? Or perhaps

The gods bestow their favors on the bad.

The gods like to favor the bad?

No! no! I have long noted malcontents

No! No! I have noticed for a long time some rebels

Who wagged their heads, and kicked against the yoke,

Who shook their heads and defied authority,

Misliking these my orders, and my rule.

Disliking my orders and my rule.

'Tis they, I warrant, who suborned my guards

It's they, I'll bet, who won over my guards

By bribes. Of evils current upon earth

With bribes. Of all the evils on earth

The worst is money. Money 'tis that sacks

The worst is money. It's money that sacks

Cities, and drives men forth from hearth and home;

Cities, and drives men out of hearth and home;

Warps and seduces native innocence,

It twists and perverts natural innocence,

And breeds a habit of dishonesty.

And encourages dishonesty.

But they who sold themselves shall find their greed

But those who sold themselves will find their greed

Out-shot the mark, and rue it soon or late.

Has got the better of them, and they'll regret it sooner or later.

Yea, as I still revere the dread of Zeus,

Yes, as I still respect the rule of Zeus,

By Zeus I swear, except ye find and bring

I swear by Zeus, that unless you find and bring

Before my presence here the very man

Into my presence the very man

Who carried out this lawless burial,

Who performed this lawless burial,

Death for your punishment shall not suffice.

Then death will not be punishment enough for you.

Hanged on a cross, alive ye first shall make

You will be hanged on a cross, and while still alive

Confession of this outrage. This will teach you

You will confess to this outrage. That will teach you

What practices are like to serve your turn.

And give you what you deserve.

There are some villainies that bring no gain.

There are some crimes that bring no profit.

For by dishonesty the few may thrive,

Only a few do well through dishonesty,

The many come to ruin and disgrace.

Most come to ruin and disgrace.

GUARD

May I not speak, or must I turn and go

May I say something, or must I turn and go

Without a word?--

Without a word?

CREON

Begone! canst thou not see

Go! Can't you see

That e'en this question irks me?

Even the question irritates me?

GUARD

Where, my lord?

Where, my lord?

Is it thy ears that suffer, or thy heart?

Does it irritate your ears, or your heart?

CREON

Why seek to probe and find the seat of pain?

Why should I want to find exactly where it hurts?

GUARD

I gall thine ears this miscreant thy mind.

I irritate your ears, but whoever did this irritates your mind.

CREON

What an inveterate babbler! get thee gone!

What a load of drivel! Get out!

GUARD

Babbler perchance, but innocent of the crime.

Driveling perhaps, but innocent.

CREON

Twice guilty, having sold thy soul for gain.

You're doubly guilty, having sold your soul for gain.

GUARD

Alas! how sad when reasoners reason wrong.

Alas! How sad when clever men think wrongly.

CREON

Go, quibble with thy reason. If thou fail'st

Go, and stop this rubbish. If you fail

To find these malefactors, thou shalt own

The wages of ill-gotten gains is death.

To find the criminals, you will find

The price of ill-gotten gains is death.

[Exit **CREON**]

GUARD

I pray he may be found. But caught or not

(And fortune must determine that) thou never

Shalt see me here returning; that is sure.

For past all hope or thought I have escaped,

I pray he may be found. But caught or not

(And that's down to fate) you shall never

See me coming back here, that's for sure.

For I have escaped, which is more than I thought or

hoped for,

And for my safety owe the gods much thanks.

And for my safety I owe much thanks to the gods.

CHORUS

(Str. 1)

Many wonders there be,

But naught more wondrous than man;

Over the surging sea,

With a whitening south wind wan,

Through the foam of the firth,

Man makes his perilous way;

And the eldest of deities Earth

That knows not toil nor decay

Ever he furrows and scores,

As his team, year in year out,

There are many wonderful things,

But none more wonderful than man;

Over the surging sea,

With the south wind blowing,

Through the waves of the bay,

Man makes his dangerous journey;

And on the oldest of gods, Earth,

That knows no strain or decay,

He always scratches and digs,

With his horses yoked together

With breed of the yoked horse,	*As a team,*
The ploughshare turneth about.	*Turning round the plough.*

(Ant. 1)

The light-witted birds of the air,	*The empty headed birds of the air,*
The beasts of the weald and the wood	*The beasts of the fields and woods,*
He traps with his woven snare,	*He can catch with his woven nets,*
And the brood of the briny flood.	*And the same for the fish in the waters.*
Master of cunning he:	*He is the master of cunning:*
The savage bull, and the hart	*The savage bull, and the deer*
Who roams the mountain free,	*Who roam free on the mountains,*
Are tamed by his infinite art;	*Are tamed by his ultimate skill;*
And the shaggy rough-maned steed	*And the shaggy rough maned horse*
Is broken to bear the bit.	*Is broken to obey the reins.*

(Str. 2)

Speech and the wind-swift speed	*Speech, and the speed*
of counsel and civic wit,	*Of wisdom and laws,*
He hath learnt for himself all these;	*He has learnt all these for himself;*
and the arrowy rain to fly	*And the arrowing rain that flies*
And the nipping airs that freeze,	*And the freezing air*
'neath the open winter sky.	*Beneath the open winter sky,*
He hath provision for all:	*He can deal with them all:*
fell plague he hath learnt to endure;	*He has learned to cope with terrible illness,*
Safe whate'er may befall:	*He can cope with anything,*
Yet for death he hath found no cure.	*But he hasn't found a cure for death.*

(Ant. 2)

Passing the wildest flight though	*Greater than the fastest flight though*
are the cunning and skill,	*Is the cunning and skill*
That guide man now to the light,	*That sometimes leads man to the light*
but now to counsels of ill.	*But sometimes towards evil.*
If he honors the laws of the land,	*If he follows the law*
and reveres the gods of the State	*And respects the gods of the State*
Proudly his city shall stand;	*His city shall stand proud;*
but a cityless outcast I rate	*But a cityless exile is the man*
Whoso bold in his pride from the path	*Who from his pride*
of right doth depart;	*Leaves the path of righteousness.*
Ne'er may I sit by his side,	*I hope I never sit next to him.*
or share the thoughts of his heart.	*Or know what goes on in his heart.*
What strange vision meets my eyes,	*What's this strange sight I see,*
Fills me with a wild surprise?	*Which fills me with astonishment?*
Sure I know her, sure 'tis she,	*Sure, I know her, it's her,*
The maid Antigone.	*The maid Antigone,*
Hapless child of hapless sire,	*Unfortunate child of an unfortunate father,*
Didst thou recklessly conspire,	*Did you recklessly plot,*
Madly brave the King's decree?	*Madly go against the King's orders?*
Therefore are they haling thee?	*Is that why they're dragging you?*

[Enter **GUARD** bringing **ANTIGONE**]

GUARD

Here is the culprit taken in the act

Of giving burial. But where's the King?

CHORUS

There from the palace he returns in time.

[Enter **CREON**]

CREON

Why is my presence timely? What has chanced?

GUARD

No man, my lord, should make a vow, for if

He ever swears he will not do a thing,

His afterthoughts belie his first resolve.

When from the hail-storm of thy threats I fled

I swore thou wouldst not see me here again;

But the wild rapture of a glad surprise

Intoxicates, and so I'm here forsworn.

And here's my prisoner, caught in the very act,

Decking the grave. No lottery this time;

This prize is mine by right of treasure-trove.

So take her, judge her, rack her, if thou wilt.

She's thine, my liege; but I may rightly claim

Hence to depart well quit of all these ills.

Here is the culprit, caught in the act

Of giving burial. But where's the King?

There he is, coming back from the palace just in time.

Just in time for what? What has happened?

No man, my lord, should make a vow, for if

He swears he won't do something

You can be sure he'll change his mind afterwards.

When I ran from the hailstorm of your threats

I swore that you would not see me here again;

But the excitement of a bit of good luck

Is intoxicating, so I'm here against my vow.

And here's my prisoner, caught in the act,

Decorating the grave. No drawing lots this time,

This prize is mine by right of finding.

So, take her, judge her, torture her, if you will.

She's yours, my king, but I can justly claim

That I can leave here without a stain on my character.

CREON

Say, how didst thou arrest the maid, and where?

Tell me how you arrested the girl, and where.

GUARD

Burying the man. There's nothing more to tell.

Burying the man. That's all that needs saying.

CREON

Hast thou thy wits? Or know'st thou what thou say'st?

Have you gone mad? Do you know what you're saying?

GUARD

I saw this woman burying the corpse

Against thy orders. Is that clear and plain?

I saw this woman burying the corpse

Against your orders. Is that plain enough?

CREON

But how was she surprised and caught in the act?

But how was she caught in the act?

GUARD

It happened thus. No sooner had we come,

Driven from thy presence by those awful threats,

Than straight we swept away all trace of dust,

And bared the clammy body. Then we sat

This is how it happened. No sooner had we got there,

Driven away from you by your awful threats,

Than we at once swept away all traces of dust

And uncovered the slimy body. Then we sat

High on the ridge to windward of the stench,

While each man kept he fellow alert and rated

Roundly the sluggard if he chanced to nap.

So all night long we watched, until the sun

Stood high in heaven, and his blazing beams

Smote us. A sudden whirlwind then upraised

A cloud of dust that blotted out the sky,

And swept the plain, and stripped the woodlands bare,

And shook the firmament. We closed our eyes

And waited till the heaven-sent plague should pass.

At last it ceased, and lo! there stood this maid.

A piercing cry she uttered, sad and shrill,

As when the mother bird beholds her nest

Robbed of its nestlings; even so the maid

Wailed as she saw the body stripped and bare,

And cursed the ruffians who had done this deed.

Anon she gathered handfuls of dry dust,

Then, holding high a well-wrought brazen urn,

Thrice on the dead she poured a lustral stream.

We at the sight swooped down on her and seized

Our quarry. Undismayed she stood, and when

We taxed her with the former crime and this,

She disowned nothing. I was glad--and grieved;

For 'tis most sweet to 'scape oneself scot-free,

And yet to bring disaster to a friend

Is grievous. Take it all in all, I deem

A man's first duty is to serve himself.

High on the ridge upwind of the stench,

While each man kept his mate awake and loudly

Abused the slacker if he happened to drop off.

So we watched all night, until the sun

Was high in the sky, with his blazing beams

Beating down on us. A sudden whirlwind then whipped up

A cloud of dust that blotted out the sky,

Swept across the plain, tore the leaves from the trees,

And shook the sky. We closed our eyes

And waited for this assault from heaven to finish.

At last it did and lo! there stood this girl.

She gave a piercing cry, sad and shrill,

Like a mother bird which sees its nest

Robbed of its chicks; this was how the girl

Wailed as she saw the body stripped and bare,

And she cursed the ruffians who had done it.

Soon she gathered handfuls of dry dust,

Then, holding up a well made bronze jug,

She poured three streams of water on the dead man.

At the sight we leapt on her and grabbed

Our prey. She stood unworried, and when

We accused her of the previous crime and this

She denied nothing. I was happy – and sad;

It's sweet to escape punishment oneself,

But to bring disaster on a friend

Is bad. But all in all, I think

A man's first duty is to look after himself.

CREON

Speak, girl, with head bent low and downcast eyes,   *Speak, girl, with your head bent low and downcast eyes,*

Does thou plead guilty or deny the deed?   *Do you plead guilty or deny it?*

ANTIGONE

Guilty. I did it, I deny it not.   *Guilty, I don't deny it.*

CREON (to **GUARD**)

Sirrah, begone whither thou wilt, and thank   *Sir, go where you want, and thank*

Thy luck that thou hast 'scaped a heavy charge.   *Your lucky stars that you've escaped a serious charge.*

(To **ANTIGONE**)   *(To **ANTIGONE**)*

Now answer this plain question, yes or no,   *Now, answer this simple question, yes or no;*

Wast thou acquainted with the interdict?   *Did you know about the order?*

ANTIGONE

I knew, all knew; how should I fail to know?   *I knew, I knew everything; how could I not know?*

CREON

And yet wert bold enough to break the law?   *And yet you were bold enough to break the law?*

ANTIGONE

Yea, for these laws were not ordained of Zeus,	*Yes, for these are not the laws of Zeus,*
And she who sits enthroned with gods below,	*And Justice, who sits on her throne at his feet,*
Justice, enacted not these human laws.	*Did not make these human laws.*
Nor did I deem that thou, a mortal man,	*Nor did I consider that you, a mortal man,*
Could'st by a breath annul and override	*Could as you chose cancel and overrule*
The immutable unwritten laws of Heaven.	*The unchangeable unwritten laws of Heaven.*
They were not born today nor yesterday;	*They were not made today or yesterday;*
They die not; and none knoweth whence they sprang.	*They never die, and nobody knows where they come from.*
I was not like, who feared no mortal's frown,	*I do not fear the displeasure of any mortal man, so I wasn't going*
To disobey these laws and so provoke	*To disobey these laws and so provoke*
The wrath of Heaven. I knew that I must die,	*Heaven's anger. I knew I must die sometime,*
E'en hadst thou not proclaimed it; and if death	*Even if you hadn't ordered it; if by this death*
Is thereby hastened, I shall count it gain.	*Comes quicker, that will please me.*
For death is gain to him whose life, like mine,	*For death is a pleasure to one whose life, like mine,*
Is full of misery. Thus my lot appears	*Is full of sorrow. So my situation seems*
Not sad, but blissful; for had I endured	*Not sad, but full of joy: if I had tolerated*
To leave my mother's son unburied there,	*Leaving my mother's son there unburied*
I should have grieved with reason, but not now.	*I would have a reason to be sad, but now I have not.*
And if in this thou judgest me a fool,	*And if you say this makes me a fool,*
Methinks the judge of folly's not acquit.	*I say that proves you're a fool yourself.*

CHORUS

A stubborn daughter of a stubborn sire,

This ill-starred maiden kicks against the pricks.

A stubborn daughter of a stubborn father,

This unfortunate girl tries to hit back at her punisher.

CREON

Well, let her know the stubbornest of wills

Are soonest bended, as the hardest iron,

O'er-heated in the fire to brittleness,

Flies soonest into fragments, shivered through.

Well, she will learn that the most stubborn wills

Are the easiest to bend, just as the hardest iron,

Overheated in the fire until it's brittle,

Is the one that is quickest to break into fragments when

it's beaten.

A snaffle curbs the fieriest steed, and he

Who in subjection lives must needs be meek.

But this proud girl, in insolence well-schooled,

First overstepped the established law, and then--

A second and worse act of insolence--

She boasts and glories in her wickedness.

Now if she thus can flout authority

Unpunished, I am woman, she the man.

But though she be my sister's child or nearer

Of kin than all who worship at my hearth,

Nor she nor yet her sister shall escape

The utmost penalty, for both I hold,

As arch-conspirators, of equal guilt.

Bring forth the older; even now I saw her

Within the palace, frenzied and distraught.

The workings of the mind discover oft

Dark deeds in darkness schemed, before the act.

More hateful still the miscreant who seeks

A bit calms the liveliest horse, and he

Who is under another's power must be humble.

But this proud girl, well taught in insolence,

First broke the law of the land, and then –

A second and more insolent act –

Boasts and celebrates her wickedness.

Now if she was allowed to do these things

Unpunished, I'm the woman and she the man.

But though she is my sister's child, and closer

Family than any of my household,

Neither she nor her sister will escape

The ultimate penalty, for I judge that they are both,

As co-conspirators, equally guilty.

Bring out the older one; just now I saw her

Inside the palace, wild and upset.

The workings of the mind often show

The dark secret deeds, before they are done.

More horrible still is the criminal who tries,

When caught, to make a virtue of a crime.

When caught, to make a virtue of the crime.

ANTIGONE

Would'st thou do more than slay thy prisoner?

Are you going to do more than kill your prisoner?

CREON

Not I, thy life is mine, and that's enough.

No, your life is mine and that's enough.

ANTIGONE

Why dally then? To me no word of thine

Is pleasant: god forbid it e'er should please;

Nor am I more acceptable to thee.

And yet how otherwise had I achieved

A name so glorious as by burying

A brother? so my townsmen all would say,

Where they not gagged by terror,

Manifold a king's prerogatives, and not the least

That all his acts and all his words are law.

Why are you waiting then? There's no word of yours

That is pleasant to me; god forbid it ever would be,

And you hate me just as much.

But how else could I have got such a great reputation,

If it wasn't for this act of burying my brother?

That's what all the townspeople would say,

If they weren't gagged by terror.

A king has many privileges, and one of the greatest

Is that all his acts and all his words are law.

CREON

Of all these Thebans none so deems but thou.

You're the only one in Thebes who thinks like this.

ANTIGONE

These think as I, but bate their breath to thee.

They all think like me, but hold their tongues around you.

CREON

Hast thou no shame to differ from all these?

You don't think your shame makes you different to them?

ANTIGONE

To reverence kith and kin can bring no shame.

To respect one's family is not shameful.

CREON

Was his dead foeman not thy kinsman too?

Wasn't his dead enemy your family too?

ANTIGONE

One mother bare them and the self-same sire.

One mother carried them and they had the same father.

CREON

Why cast a slur on one by honoring one?

So why insult one by honoring the other?

ANTIGONE

The dead man will not bear thee out in this.

The dead man would not think like you.

CREON

Surely, if good and evil fare alive.

I'm sure you're right, if good and evil still exist.

ANTIGONE

The slain man was no villain but a brother.

That dead man was no villain but my brother.

CREON

The patriot perished by the outlaw's brand.

The patriot was killed with the outlaw's weapon.

ANTIGONE

Nathless the realms below these rites require.

Whatever, the underworld requires these ceremonies.

CREON

Not that the base should fare as do the brave.

They don't require that scum should be treated the same as the brave.

ANTIGONE

Who knows if this world's crimes are virtues there?

Who knows, maybe crimes in this world are good deeds there.

CREON

Not even death can make a foe a friend.

Not even death can make an enemy a friend.

ANTIGONE

My nature is for mutual love, not hate.

I lean towards love, not hatred.

CREON

Die then, and love the dead if thou must;

Die then, and love the dead if you want;

No woman shall be the master while I live.

No woman shall be master whilst I'm alive.

[Enter **ISMENE**]

CHORUS

Lo from out the palace gate,

Look, from the doors of the palace,

Weeping o'er her sister's fate,

Here comes Isemene, weeping

Comes Ismene; see her brow,

For her sister's fate; see her brow,

Once serene, beclouded now,

Once so serene, now frowning,

See her beauteous face o'erspread

And her lovely face is covered

With a flush of angry red.

With an angry red flush.

CREON

Woman, who like a viper unperceived

The woman who, like an unseen viper,

Didst harbor in my house and drain my blood,

Hid in my house and drained my blood.

Two plagues I nurtured blindly, so it proved,

It seems I nourished two curses

To sap my throne. Say, didst thou too abet

To attack my throne. Tell me, did you help

This crime, or dost abjure all privity?

In this crime, or do you deny all knowledge?

ISMENE

I did the deed, if she will have it so,

And with my sister claim to share the guilt.

I did the deed, if she says so,

And I will share the guilt with my sister.

ANTIGONE

That were unjust. Thou would'st not act with me

At first, and I refused thy partnership.

That would not be fair. You wouldn't help me

At first, and I rejected your partnership.

ISMENE

But now thy bark is stranded, I am bold

To claim my share as partner in the loss.

But now you are caught, I feel strengthened

To claim an equal share of punishment.

ANTIGONE

Who did the deed the under-world knows well:

A friend in word is never friend of mine.

Who did this the underworld knows;

Someone who's friendly in words not deeds is no friend

of mine.

ISMENE

O sister, scorn me not, let me but share

Thy work of piety, and with thee die.

Oh sister, do not reject me, but let me share

Your good deed, and die with you.

ANTIGONE

Claim not a work in which thou hadst no hand;

Don't claim a deed you weren't involved in;

One death sufficeth. Wherefore should'st thou die?

One death is enough. Why should you die?

ISMENE

What would life profit me bereft of thee?

What could life offer me if you're gone?

ANTIGONE

Ask Creon, he's thy kinsman and best friend.

Ask Creon, he's your family and best friend.

ISMENE

Why taunt me? Find'st thou pleasure in these gibes?

Why do you taunt me? Do you enjoy causing me pain?

ANTIGONE

'Tis a sad mockery, if indeed I mock.

It's a sad joke, if indeed I'm joking.

ISMENE

O say if I can help thee even now.

Say if there's any help I can give, even now.

ANTIGONE

No, save thyself; I grudge not thy escape.

No, save yourself; I don't begrudge you escaping.

ISMENE

Is e'en this boon denied, to share thy lot?

Will you refuse even this favor, that I should share your fate?

ANTIGONE

Yea, for thou chosed'st life, and I to die.

Yes, for you chose life and I chose death.

ISMENE

Thou canst not say that I did not protest.

You can't say I didn't tell you not to.

ANTIGONE

Well, some approved thy wisdom, others mine.

Well, some agreed with you, some with me.

ISMENE

But now we stand convicted, both alike.

But now we are both convicted, just the same.

ANTIGONE

Fear not; thou livest, I died long ago
Then when I gave my life to save the dead.

*Do not fear; you live, I died long before
I gave my life to save the dead.*

CREON

Both maids, methinks, are crazed. One suddenly

Has lost her wits, the other was born mad.

Both girls, I think, are mad. One has just

Lost her mind, the other was born mad.

ISMENE

Yea, so it falls, sire, when misfortune comes,

The wisest even lose their mother wit.

Yes my lord, when misfortune comes

Even the wisest can lose their minds.

CREON

I' faith thy wit forsook thee when thou mad'st

Thy choice with evil-doers to do ill.

You lost your mind when you decided

To become a criminal.

ISMENE

What life for me without my sister here?

What life is there for me if I don't have my sister?

CREON

Say not thy sister here: thy sister's dead.

Don't talk as if your sister's here; she's dead.

ISMENE

What, wilt thou slay thy own son's plighted bride?

What, will you kill your son's fiancée?

CREON

Aye, let him raise him seed from other fields.

Yes, he can plough a different field.

ISMENE

No new espousal can be like the old

No new engagement could match the first one.

CREON

A plague on trulls who court and woo our sons.

Curse these sluts who chase and seduce our sons.

ANTIGONE

O Haemon, how thy sire dishonors thee!

Oh Haemon, how your father insults you!

CREON

A plague on thee and thy accursed bride!

A curse on you and your damned bride!

CHORUS

What, wilt thou rob thine own son of his bride?

What, will you take your son's bride from him?

CREON

'Tis death that bars this marriage, not his sire.

It's death that will stop this marriage, not his father.

CHORUS

So her death-warrant, it would seem, is sealed.

So her death warrant is sealed, it seems.

CREON

By you, as first by me; off with them, guards,

By you, as it was first by me. Take them away, guards,

And keep them close. Henceforward let them learn

And keep a close eye on them. From now on let them learn

To live as women use, not roam at large.

To live as women should, not wandering about the world.

For e'en the bravest spirits run away

Even the bravest might try to run

When they perceive death pressing on life's heels.

When they see death snapping at their heels.

CHORUS

(Str. 1)

Thrice blest are they who never tasted pain!

The ones who have never known pain are triply blessed!

If once the curse of Heaven attaint a race,

If the curse of heaven lands once on a family,

The infection lingers on and speeds apace,

The stain stays and quickly spreads,

Age after age, and each the cup must drain.

Age after age, so all must suffer.

So when Etesian blasts from Thrace downpour

Like when the Etesian winds send storms from Thrace,

Sweep o'er the blackening main and whirl to land

Sweeping over the darkened sea and whirlpools to land,

From Ocean's cavernous depths his ooze and sand,

From the great depths of the ocean its ooze and sand

Billow on billow thunders on the shore.

Crashes on the shore in wave after wave.

(Ant. 1)

On the Labdacidae I see descending	*I see sorrow on sorrow descending*
Woe upon woe; from days of old some god	*On the family of Labacidus, from ancient times some god*
Laid on the race a malison, and his rod	*Laid a curse on the family, and his stick*
Scourges each age with sorrows never ending.	*Beats each generation with endless sorrows.*
The light that dawned upon its last born son	*The light that shone on its last son*
Is vanished, and the bloody axe of Fate	*Has gone out, and the bloody axe of fate*
Has felled the goodly tree that blossomed late.	*Has cut down that fine tree that used to blossom.*
O Oedipus, by reckless pride undone!	*Oh Oedipus, brought down by your reckless pride!*

(Str. 2)

Thy might, O Zeus, what mortal power can quell?	*What mortal power can fight against you, oh Zeus?*
Not sleep that lays all else beneath its spell,	*Not sleep that overcomes everything else,*
Nor moons that never tier: untouched by Time,	*Nor the moons that never tire: time cannot touch you,*
Throned in the dazzling light	*On your throne in the dazzling light*
That crowns Olympus' height,	*On the peak of Olympus,*
Thou reignest King, omnipotent, sublime.	*You reign as the all-powerful perfect King.*
Past, present, and to be,	*Past, present and future,*
All bow to thy decree,	*All bow to your orders;*
All that exceeds the mean by Fate	*Anything that rises above the common herd*
Is punished, Love or Hate.	*Is punished by fate, whether it's love or hate.*

(Ant. 2)

Hope flits about never-wearying wings;	*Hope is always present, tireless,*
Profit to some, to some light loves she brings,	*She brings some wealth, some light love,*

But no man knoweth how her gifts may turn,

Till 'neath his feet the treacherous ashes burn.

Sure 'twas a sage inspired that spake this word;

If_evil_good_appear

To_any,_Fate_is_near;

And brief the respite from her flaming sword.

Hither comes in angry mood

Haemon, latest of thy brood;

Is it for his bride he's grieved,

Or her marriage-bed deceived,

Doth he make his mourn for thee,

Maid forlorn, Antigone?

But nobody knows how her gifts can change

So that he'll suddenly be in hell.

It was an inspired wise man who said,

"If evil looks like good to anyone,

Then fate is waiting for them,

And they won't escape her punishment for long."

Here comes Haemon, your youngest,

And he is in an angry mood;

Is he sad for his bride,

Or the marriage he's cheated of;

Is he mourning for you,

Sad Antigone?

[Enter **HAEMON**]

CREON

Soon shall we know, better than seer can tell.

Learning may fixed decree anent thy bride,

Thou mean'st not, son, to rave against thy sire?

Know'st not whate'er we do is done in love?

We'll soon know, better than any prophet can tell us;

Learning that the law has condemned your bride,

You don't intend, son, to blame your father?

Don't you know that everything I do is done from love?

HAEMON

O father, I am thine, and I will take

Thy wisdom as the helm to steer withal.

Therefore no wedlock shall by me be held

More precious than thy loving goverance.

Oh father, I am your servant, and I will take

Your wisdom as my guide.

So no marriage is more important to me

Than your loving rule.

CREON

Well spoken: so right-minded sons should feel,   *Well said: this is how right-minded sons should behave,*

In all deferring to a father's will.   *Always bowing to their father's orders.*

For 'tis the hope of parents they may rear   *All parents hope that they will raise*

A brood of sons submissive, keen to avenge   *Sons who are obedient, keen to avenge*

Their father's wrongs, and count his friends their own.   *The wrongs done to their father, and count his friends as theirs.*

But who begets unprofitable sons,   *But the one who breeds ungrateful sons,*

He verily breeds trouble for himself,   *He truly breeds trouble for himself,*

And for his foes much laughter. Son, be warned   *And makes his enemies laugh. Son, be warned,*

And let no woman fool away thy wits.   *And never let a woman fool with your mind.*

Ill fares the husband mated with a shrew,   *The husband married to a nagging woman is in trouble,*

And her embraces very soon wax cold.   *And her embraces will soon lose their warmth.*

For what can wound so surely to the quick   *For what cuts to the quick quite as much*

As a false friend? So spue and cast her off,   *As a false friend? So spit her out and throw her out,*

Bid her go find a husband with the dead.   *Tell her to go and find a husband in hell.*

For since I caught her openly rebelling,   *For as I've caught her in open rebellion,*

Of all my subjects the one malcontent,   *The one malcontent amongst all my subjects,*

I will not prove a traitor to the State.   *I will not be a traitor to the State.*

She surely dies. Go, let her, if she will,   *She must die. Let her, if she wants,*

Appeal to Zeus the god of Kindred, for   *Appeal to Zeus, the god of family, for*

If thus I nurse rebellion in my house,   *If I allow rebellion inside my house*

Shall not I foster mutiny without?   *Surely that will lead to rebellion outside.*

For whoso rules his household worthily,   *The one who rules his own household well*

Will prove in civic matters no less wise.   *Will prove to be a good ruler of a city.*

But he who overbears the laws, or thinks   *But he who ignores the law, or thinks*

To overrule his rulers, such as one

I never will allow. Whome'er the State

Appoints must be obeyed in everything,

But small and great, just and unjust alike.

I warrant such a one in either case

Would shine, as King or subject; such a man

Would in the storm of battle stand his ground,

A comrade leal and true; but Anarchy--

What evils are not wrought by Anarchy!

She ruins States, and overthrows the home,

She dissipates and routs the embattled host;

While discipline preserves the ordered ranks.

Therefore we must maintain authority

And yield to title to a woman's will.

Better, if needs be, men should cast us out

Than hear it said, a woman proved his match.

He can ignore his rulers, that

I will never allow. Whoever the State

Chooses to lead must be obeyed in everything,

Big or small, just or unjust alike.

I say a man like this would be great,

Either as a King or a subject; such a man

Would stand his ground in the storm of battle,

A loyal and true comrade; but anarchy –

What evils anarchy does!

She ruins States and destroys the home,

She spoils and defeats armies;

While discipline keeps the ranks in order.

So we must keep our authority

And not allow a woman's wishes to outrank the law.

It would be better if men would throw me out

Than to hear it said, he was beaten by a woman.

CHORUS

To me, unless old age have dulled wits,

Thy words appear both reasonable and wise.

To me, unless old age has made me stupid,

Your words seem reasonable and wise.

HAEMON

Father, the gods implant in mortal men

Reason, the choicest gift bestowed by heaven.

'Tis not for me to say thou errest, nor

Would I arraign thy wisdom, if I could;

Father, the gods give mortal men

Reason, the greatest gift heaven has.

It's not for me to say you're wrong, and

I wouldn't find fault with your wisdom if I could;

And yet wise thoughts may come to other men	*And yet other men can have wise thoughts too,*
And, as thy son, it falls to me to mark	*And, as your son, it's my duty to note*
The acts, the words, the comments of the crowd.	*The acts, the words, the comments of the crowd.*
The commons stand in terror of thy frown,	*The public are terrified of your anger,*
And dare not utter aught that might offend,	*And dare not say anything that might offend you,*
But I can overhear their muttered plaints,	*But I have overheard their muttered complaints*
Know how the people mourn this maiden doomed	*And know how they mourn this girl, sentenced*
For noblest deeds to die the worst of deaths.	*To the worst sort of death for her noblest actions.*
When her own brother slain in battle lay	*When her own brother, killed in battle, lay*
Unsepulchered, she suffered not his corse	*Unburied, she did not let his corpse*
To lie for carrion birds and dogs to maul:	*Lie out for the dogs and carrion birds:*
Should not her name (they cry) be writ in gold?	*They ask why her name isn't praised as high as possible.*
Such the low murmurings that reach my ear.	*These are the rumblings I hear.*
O father, nothing is by me more prized	*Oh father, nothing is more important to me*
Than thy well-being, for what higher good	*Than your wellbeing, for what better thing*
Can children covet than their sire's fair fame,	*Can a child want than a great reputation for their father,*
As fathers too take pride in glorious sons?	*Just as fathers want the same thing for their sons?*
Therefore, my father, cling not to one mood,	*So, father, don't stick to a fixed path,*
And deemed not thou art right, all others wrong.	*Thinking you're right and all others are wrong.*
For whoso thinks that wisdom dwells with him,	*For the person who thinks that he is wise,*
That he alone can speak or think aright,	*Thinking that he's the only one who speaks or thinks the truth,*
Such oracles are empty breath when tried.	*Such thoughts are empty when tested.*
The wisest man will let himself be swayed	*The wisest man will let himself be influenced*
By others' wisdom and relax in time.	*By the wisdom of others, and change his position in time.*
See how the trees beside a stream in flood	*See how the trees by a flooding stream*
Save, if they yield to force, each spray unharmed,	*Survive, if they bend with the force, every flower untouched,*

But by resisting perish root and branch.

The mariner who keeps his mainsheet taut,

And will not slacken in the gale, is like

To sail with thwarts reversed, keel uppermost.

Relent then and repent thee of thy wrath;

For, if one young in years may claim some sense,

I'll say 'tis best of all to be endowed

With absolute wisdom; but, if that's denied,

(And nature takes not readily that ply)

Next wise is he who lists to sage advice.

But by resisting the whole tree falls.

The sailor who keeps his mainsail tight

And will not loosen it when gales blow, is likely

To find his ship overturned.

So relent and give up your anger;

For, if one young in years might claim to have some sense,

I'll say the best thing is to have

Perfect wisdom, but, if that's not given,

(And nature doesn't often give such riches)

The next best thing is to listen to good advice.

CHORUS

If he says aught in season, heed him, King.

If you think his words are to the point, then listen to him, King.

(To **HAEMON**)

*(To **HAEMON**)*

Heed thou thy sire too; both have spoken well.

You listen to your father as well; you have both spoken well.

CREON

What, would you have us at our age be schooled,

Lessoned in prudence by a beardless boy?

What, do you think at my age I should be taught,

Lectured in judgment by a beardless boy?

HAEMON

I plead for justice, father, nothing more.

I am asking for justice, father, that's all.

Weigh me upon my merit, not my years.

Judge me on my merits, not my youth.

CREON

Strange merit this to sanction lawlessness!

It's a strange merit this, to want to allow her to break the law!

HAEMON

For evil-doers I would urge no plea.

I wouldn't speak up for real criminals.

CREON

Is not this maid an arrant law-breaker?

And isn't this girl a confirmed criminal?

HAEMON

The Theban commons with one voice say, No.

The Theban people unanimously say, no.

CREON

What, shall the mob dictate my policy?

What, shall the mob dictate my policies?

HAEMON

'Tis thou, methinks, who speakest like a boy.

It's you, I think, who's talking like a child.

CREON

Am I to rule for others, or myself?

Am I to do what I think right or what others tell me?

HAEMON

A State for one man is no State at all.

A State that is only the will of one man is no State at all.

CREON

The State is his who rules it, so 'tis held.

The State belongs to its ruler, that is the custom.

HAEMON

As monarch of a desert thou wouldst shine.

So you would be good as king over a desert.

CREON

This boy, methinks, maintains the woman's cause.

I think this boy supports the woman's cause.

HAEMON

If thou be'st woman, yes. My thought's for thee.

Only if you're a woman. I'm thinking of you.

CREON

O reprobate, would'st wrangle with thy sire?

You scoundrel, are you going to argue with your father?

HAEMON

Because I see thee wrongfully perverse.

Because I see that you're being deliberately stubborn, and wrong.

CREON

And am I wrong, if I maintain my rights?

Am I wrong to insist on my rights?

HAEMON

Talk not of rights; thou spurn'st the due of Heaven.

Don't talk about rights; you are going against Heaven.

CREON

O heart corrupt, a woman's minion thou!

You have had your heart turned, you're a slave to a woman!

HAEMON

Slave to dishonor thou wilt never find me.

But you'll never find me a slave to dishonor.

CREON

Thy speech at least was all a plea for her.

What you said was all pleading for her.

HAEMON

And thee and me, and for the gods below.

And for you, me, and the gods of the underworld.

CREON

Living the maid shall never be thy bride.

The girl will never live to be your bride.

HAEMON

So she shall die, but one will die with her.

So she'll die, but someone else will die with her.

CREON

Hast come to such a pass as threaten me?

Has it come to this, that you are threatening me?

HAEMON

What threat is this, vain counsels to reprove?

How is it threatening to criticize bad judgment?

CREON

Vain fool to instruct thy betters; thou shall rue it.

You're a vain fool to lecture your superiors; you shall regret it.

HAEMON

Wert not my father, I had said thou err'st.

If you weren't my father I'd say you're wrong.

CREON

Play not the spaniel, thou a woman's slave.

Don't be a lapdog, you woman's slave.

HAEMON

When thou dost speak, must no man make reply?

So when you speak nobody can answer?

CREON

This passes bounds. By heaven, thou shalt not rate

And jeer and flout me with impunity.

Off with the hateful thing that she may die

At once, beside her bridegroom, in his sight.

This is beyond belief. By god, you will not scold

And mock and disobey me without punishment.

Take that horrid thing away so she can die

At once, in the sight of her bridegroom, at his side.

HAEMON

Think not that in my sight the maid shall die,

Or by my side; never shalt thou again

Behold my face hereafter. Go, consort

With friends who like a madman for their mate.

Don't think the girl will die in my sight,

Or by my side; you shall never again

See my face from now on. Go and hang out with

People who want a madman for their friend.

[Exit **HAEMON**]

CHORUS

Thy son has gone, my liege, in angry haste.

Your son has gone, my lord, with angry haste.

Fell is the wrath of youth beneath a smart.

The anger of youth when reprimanded is fierce.

CREON

Let him go vent his fury like a fiend:

These sisters twain he shall not save from death.

Let him go and blow off steam like a devil;

He won't save these two sisters from death.

CHORUS

Surely, thou meanest not to slay them both?

Surely, you don't mean to kill them both?

CREON

I stand corrected; only her who touched

The body.

I stand corrected; only the one who touched

The body.

CHORUS

And what death is she to die?

And how is he to die?

CREON

She shall be taken to some desert place

By man untrod, and in a rock-hewn cave,

With food no more than to avoid the taint

That homicide might bring on all the State,

Buried alive. There let her call in aid

The King of Death, the one god she reveres,

She'll be taken to some deserted place

Where no man goes, and in a rocky cave,

With just enough food to avoid the stain

That murder might bring on the State,

Buried alive. There she can call for help from

The King of Death, the one god she respects,

Or learn too late a lesson learnt at last:

'Tis labor lost, to reverence the dead.

Or she can learn the lesson, too late,

That it's a waste of effort to worship the dead.

CHORUS

(Str.)

Love resistless in fight,

all yield at a glance of thine eye,

Love who pillowed all night

on a maiden's cheek dost lie,

Over the upland holds.

Shall mortals not yield to thee?

Love cannot be resisted,

All surrender at a glance from you,

Love who lies all night

On a maiden's cheek,

Love holds all the cards.

Shouldn't men give in to you?

(Ant).

Mad are thy subjects all,

and even the wisest heart

Straight to folly will fall,

at a touch of thy poisoned dart.

Thou didst kindle the strife,

this feud of kinsman with kin,

By the eyes of a winsome wife,

and the yearning her heart to win.

For as her consort still,

enthroned with Justice above,

Thou bendest man to thy will,

O all invincible Love.

All you rule over are mad,

And even the wisest heart

Will become stupid at once,

When touched by your poisoned dart.

You started this fight,

This feud of blood on blood,

With the eyes of a charming wife.

And the desire to win her heart.

As the one who is joined

With the gods, next to Justice,

You make men do what you want,

All-powerful Love.

Lo I myself am borne aside,

From Justice, as I view this bride.

(O sight an eye in tears to drown)

Antigone, so young, so fair,

Thus hurried down

Death's bower with the dead to share.

Look, I myself am led away

From Justice, when I look at this bride.

This is a sight which drowns the eyes in tears,

Antigone, so young, so lovely,

Rushed away

Into the home of the dead.

ANTIGONE

Friends, countrymen, my last farewell I make;

My journey's done.

One last fond, lingering, longing look I take

At the bright sun.

For Death who puts to sleep both young and old

Hales my young life,

And beckons me to Acheron's dark fold,

An unwed wife.

No youths have sung the marriage song for me,

My bridal bed

No maids have strewn with flowers from the lea,

'Tis Death I wed.

Friends, countrymen, I make my last goodbye;

My journey is over.

I take one last sweet, lingering, longing look

At the bright sun.

For Death who can put to sleep both young and old

Drags my young life away,

And calls me down to the underworld,

An unmarried wife.

No youths have sung the marriage song for me,

My bridal bed

Has not been covered by girls with meadow flowers;

It's Death I'm marrying.

CHORUS

But bethink thee, thou art sped,

Great and glorious, to the dead.

Thou the sword's edge hast not tasted,

No disease thy frame hath wasted.

But think, you are going

To the underworld with glory.

You haven't been cut by a sword

Or ravaged by disease.

Freely thou alone shalt go

Living to the dead below.

You are going unsullied

To the dead below.

ANTIGONE

Nay, but the piteous tale I've heard men tell

Of Tantalus' doomed child,

Chained upon Siphylus' high rocky fell,

That clung like ivy wild,

Drenched by the pelting rain and whirling snow,

Left there to pine,

While on her frozen breast the tears aye flow--

Her fate is mine.

No, I've heard the sad tale told

Of the doomed child of Tantalus,

Chained up high on the rock slopes of Siphylus,

Clinging to it like wild ivy,

Soaked by the pelting rain and whirling snow,

Left there to waste away

While the tears fall on her cold breast forever –

That is my fate.

CHORUS

She was sprung of gods, divine,

Mortals we of mortal line.

Like renown with gods to gain

Recompenses all thy pain.

Take this solace to thy tomb

Hers in life and death thy doom.

She was born from the gods,

And we are mortals.

To become as famous as the gods

Will pay you for all your pain.

Take this comfort to your grave,

That you suffer her fate in life, have her fame in death.

ANTIGONE

Alack, alack! Ye mock me. Is it meet

Thus to insult me living, to my face?

Cease, by our country's altars I entreat,

Alas, alas! You are mocking me. Is it right

To insult me to my face like this while I'm still alive?

Stop it, I pray you in the name of our holy places,

Ye lordly rulers of a lordly race.

O fount of Dirce, wood-embowered plain

Where Theban chariots to victory speed,

Mark ye the cruel laws that now have wrought my bane,

The friends who show no pity in my need!

Was ever fate like mine? O monstrous doom,

Within a rock-built prison sepulchered,

To fade and wither in a living tomb,

And alien midst the living and the dead.

You lordly rulers of a lordly race.

Oh spring of Dirce, wood covered plain,

Where the Theban chariots rush to victory,

Look at the cruel laws which have damned me,

And the friends who show no pity in my trouble!

Did anyone ever have a fate like this? Oh terrible sentence,

To be entombed within a rocky prison,

Unknown to both the living and the dead.

CHORUS

(Str. 3)

In thy boldness over-rash

Madly thou thy foot didst dash

'Gainst high Justice' altar stair.

Thou a father's guild dost bear.

You were proud and hasty;

You madly kicked out

At the altar of Justice.

You carry a father's guilt.

ANTIGONE

At this thou touchest my most poignant pain,

My ill-starred father's piteous disgrace,

The taint of blood, the hereditary stain,

That clings to all of Labdacus' famed race.

Woe worth the monstrous marriage-bed where lay

A mother with the son her womb had borne,

That is what hurts me most,

My unlucky father's sad disgrace,

The stain of blood, the inherited stain,

That sticks to all of the famous family of Labadacus.

A curse on the terrible marriage bed where

A mother lay with the son she'd carried,

Therein I was conceived, woe worth the day, | *Where I was conceived, a curse on the day,*

Fruit of incestuous sheets, a maid forlorn,

And now I pass, accursed and unwed, | *And now I die, cursed and unmarried,*

To meet them as an alien there below; | *To meet them as a stranger there below;*

And thee, O brother, in marriage ill-bestead, | *And you, my brother, ill-served by marriage,*

'Twas thy dead hand that dealt me this death-blow. | *It was you, dead, who dealt me the fatal blow.*

CHORUS

Religion has her chains, 'tis true, | *Religion has her obligations, it's true,*

Let rite be paid when rites are due. | *And respect should be paid when it's due.*

Yet is it ill to disobey | *But it is bad to disobey*

The powers who hold by might the sway. | *The powers who hold authority through strength.*

Thou hast withstood authority, | *You have defied that authority,*

A self-willed rebel, thou must die. | *A willful rebel, and so you must die.*

ANTIGONE

Unwept, unwed, unfriended, hence I go, | *Unmourned, unmarried, friendless, I leave here,*

No longer may I see the day's bright eye; | *And will no longer see the sun;*

Not one friend left to share my bitter woe, | *There's not one friend left to share my bitter sorrow,*

And o'er my ashes heave one passing sigh. | *And heave just one sigh over my remains.*

CREON

If wail and lamentation aught availed | *If whining and tears could do anything*

To stave off death, I trow they'd never end. | *To keep death away, I'm sure nobody would ever stop.*

Away with her, and having walled her up | *Take her away, and having walled her up*

60

In a rock-vaulted tomb, as I ordained,	*In a rocky tomb, as I ordered,*
Leave her alone at liberty to die,	*Leave her alone, free to die or,*
Or, if she choose, to live in solitude,	*If she chooses, to live alone,*
The tomb her dwelling. We in either case	*With the tomb as her home. Either way*
Are guiltless as concerns this maiden's blood,	*We are guiltless with regard to her death,*
Only on earth no lodging shall she find.	*But she will find no home on earth.*

ANTIGONE

O grave, O bridal bower, O prison house	*Oh grave, oh bridal chamber, oh prison house,*
Hewn from the rock, my everlasting home,	*Cut from the rock, my eternal home,*
Whither I go to join the mighty host	*From where I go to join the great army*
Of kinsfolk, Persephassa's guests long dead,	*Of kinsfolk, the long dead guests of Persephassa,*
The last of all, of all more miserable,	*The last of all and the most miserable*
I pass, my destined span of years cut short.	*I go, my destined lifespan cut short.*
And yet good hope is mine that I shall find	*And yet I am hopeful that I'll find*
A welcome from my sire, a welcome too,	*A welcome from my father, a welcome, too*
From thee, my mother, and my brother dear;	*From you, my mother, and my dear brother.*
From with these hands, I laved and decked your limbs	*These hands washed and dressed your body*
In death, and poured libations on your grave.	*In death, and poured offerings on your grave.*
And last, my Polyneices, unto thee	*My Polyneices, I paid you due respect,*
I paid due rites, and this my recompense!	*And this is my reward!*
Yet am I justified in wisdom's eyes.	*But the wise know that I was right.*
For even had it been some child of mine,	*For even if you had been some child of mine,*
Or husband mouldering in death's decay,	*Or a husband lingering at death's door,*
I had not wrought this deed despite the State.	*I would not have gone against the State in this way.*
What is the law I call in aid? 'Tis thus	*Why do I say I was right then? This is how*
I argue. Had it been a husband dead	*I see it. If it had been a dead husband*

I might have wed another, and have borne

Another child, to take the dead child's place.

But, now my sire and mother both are dead,

No second brother can be born for me.

Thus by the law of conscience I was led

To honor thee, dear brother, and was judged

By Creon guilty of a heinous crime.

And now he drags me like a criminal,

A bride unwed, amerced of marriage-song

And marriage-bed and joys of motherhood,

By friends deserted to a living grave.

What ordinance of heaven have I transgressed?

Hereafter can I look to any god

For succor, call on any man for help?

Alas, my piety is impious deemed.

Well, if such justice is approved of heaven,

I shall be taught by suffering my sin;

But if the sin is theirs, O may they suffer

No worse ills than the wrongs they do to me.

I could have married again, and had

Another child, to take the dead child's place.

But my mother and father are both dead,

And no other brother can be born for me.

So by the laws of conscience I was led

To honor you, dear brother, and was judged

By Creon to be guilty of a terrible crime.

And now he drags me like a criminal,

An unwed bride, cheated of marriage song

And marriage bed and the joys of motherhood,

Left by my friends to a living grave.

What law of Heaven have I disobeyed?

After this can I look to any god

For relief, call on any man for help?

Alas, my piety is judged blasphemy.

Well, if this is the justice heaven approves,

I shall be punished for my sins;

But if the sin is theirs, may they suffer

Nothing worse than the wrongs they do me.

CHORUS

The same ungovernable will

Drives like a gale the maiden still.

That same headstrong will

Still drives the girl like a gale.

CREON

Therefore, my guards who let her stay

So, the guards who have let her stay here

Shall smart full sore for their delay.   *Shall be well punished for their delay.*

ANTIGONE

Ah, woe is me! This word I hear   *Alas! Hearing these words*

Brings death most near.   *Brings death very close.*

CHORUS

I have no comfort. What he saith,   *I can say nothing to comfort you. What he says*

Portends no other thing than death.   *Means nothing other than death.*

ANTIGONE

My fatherland, city of Thebes divine,   *My fatherland, divine city of Thebes,*

Ye gods of Thebes whence sprang my line,   *You gods of Thebes from whom my family comes.*

Look, puissant lords of Thebes, on me;   *You mighty lords of Thebes, all look on me;*

The last of all your royal house ye see.   *You see the last survivor of your royal house.*

Martyred by men of sin, undone.   *Martyred by men, overcome;*

Such meed my piety hath won.   *This is what my piety has got me.*

[Exit **ANTIGONE**]

CHORUS

(Str. 1)

Like to thee that maiden bright,   *You are like that bright maiden.*

63

Danae, in her brass-bound tower,

Once exchanged the glad sunlight

For a cell, her bridal bower.

And yet she sprang of royal line,

My child, like thine,

And nursed the seed

By her conceived

Of Zeus descending in a golden shower.

Strange are the ways of Fate, her power

Nor wealth, nor arms withstand, nor tower;

Nor brass-prowed ships, that breast the sea

From Fate can flee.

Danae, in her brass tower,

Who had to exchange the sweet sunlight

For a cell, which became her bridal chamber.

And yet she came from royal stock,

My child, like yours,

And nursed the child

She conceived

From Zeus coming to her as a golden rain.

The ways of fate are strange, her power

Cannot be resisted by wealth, or arms, or towers;

And brassclad ships, that plough through the sea,

Cannot escape fate.

(Ant. 1)

Thus Dryas' child, the rash Edonian King,

For words of high disdain

Did Bacchus to a rocky dungeon bring,

To cool the madness of a fevered brain.

His frenzy passed,

He learnt at last

'Twas madness gibes against a god to fling.

For once he fain had quenched the Maenad's fire;

And of the tuneful Nine provoked the ire.

So Dryas' child, the unwise Edonian King,

As punishment for contemptuous words

Brought Bacchus to a rocky dungeon,

To calm down the madness of his fevered brain.

His frenzy passed

And he learned

That it was madness to throw insults at a god.

Once he tried to put out the nymphs' fire,

And provoked the anger of the Muses.

(Str. 2)

By the Iron Rocks that guard the double main,

By the iron rocks that guard the two seas,

On Bosporus' lone strand,

Where stretcheth Salmydessus' plain

In the wild Thracian land,

There on his borders Ares witnessed

The vengeance by a jealous step-dame ta'en

The gore that trickled from a spindle red,

The sightless orbits of her step-sons twain.

On the lonely shore of the Bosphorus,

Where Salmydessus' plain stretched

Into the wild lands of Thrace,

There on his borders Mars saw

The revenge taken by a jealous step-mother,

The gore that trickled from a red needle,

And the sightless eyes of her two stepsons.

(Ant. 2)

Wasting away they mourned their piteous doom,

The blasted issue of their mother's womb.

But she her lineage could trace

To great Erecththeus' race;

Daughter of Boreas in her sire's vast caves

Reared, where the tempest raves,

Swift as his horses o'er the hills she sped;

A child of gods; yet she, my child, like thee,

By Destiny

That knows not death nor age--she too was vanquished.

Wasting away they mourned their horrid fate,

The cursed issue of their mother's womb.

But she could trace her heritage

To the great Erectheus;

The daughter of Boreas, she was raised

In the great caves of her father where the storms rage;

She sped as swift as horses over the fields,

A child of gods; but like you my child

She was defeated by fate

Which never grows old or dies.

[Enter **TEIRESIAS** and BOY]

TEIRESIAS

Princes of Thebes, two wayfarers as one,

Having betwixt us eyes for one, we are here.

The blind man cannot move without a guide.

Prince of Thebes, we are one traveler in two,

As we only have eyes for one; we are here.

The blind man cannot move without a guide.

CREON

Why tidings, old Teiresias?

What news, old Teiresias?

TEIRESIAS

I will tell thee;

I will tell you,

And when thou hearest thou must heed the seer.

And when you hear you must listen to the prophet.

CREON

Thus far I ne'er have disobeyed thy rede.

I've never gone against your advice.

TEIRESIAS

So hast thou steered the ship of State aright.

And that way you've governed well.

CREON

I know it, and I gladly own my debt.

I know it, and gladly admit my debt to you.

TEIRESIAS

Bethink thee that thou treadest once again

Be warned that once again

The razor edge of peril.

You are on the razor's edge of danger.

CREON

What is this?

Thy words inspire a dread presentiment.

What is this?

Your words fill me with dread.

TEIRESIAS

The divination of my arts shall tell.

Sitting upon my throne of augury,

As is my wont, where every fowl of heaven

Find harborage, upon mine ears was borne

A jargon strange of twitterings, hoots, and screams;

So knew I that each bird at the other tare

With bloody talons, for the whirr of wings

Could signify naught else. Perturbed in soul,

I straight essayed the sacrifice by fire

On blazing altars, but the god of Fire

Came not in flame, and from the thigh bones dripped

And sputtered in the ashes a foul ooze;

Gall-bladders cracked and spurted up: the fat

Melted and fell and left the thigh bones bare.

Such are the signs, taught by this lad, I read--

As I guide others, so the boy guides me--

The frustrate signs of oracles grown dumb.

O King, thy willful temper ails the State,

For all our shrines and altars are profaned

By what has filled the maw of dogs and crows,

The flesh of Oedipus' unburied son.

I shall tell you what my skills have discovered.

Sitting in my prophet's seat,

As usual, where I can hear

What all the birds are saying, I heard

A strange racket of twittering, hoots and screams;

So I knew that all the birds were tearing at each other

With bloody claws, for the whirr of wings

Could mean nothing else. Feeling perturbed

I straight away tried a fire sacrifice

On the blazing altars, but the god of Fire

Did not give flame, and from the thigh bones there dripped

And sputtered in the ashes a foul ooze;

Gall bladders cracked and spurted, the fat

Melted and fell and left the thigh bones bare.

These were the signs I read, described by this lad –

As I guide others, so this boy guides me –

The frustrating signs of oracles gone quiet.

Oh King, your headstrong temper is harming the State,

For all our shrines and altars have been polluted

By the vomit of dogs and crows,

The flesh of Oedipus' unburied son.

Therefore the angry gods abominate	*Because of this the angry gods reject*
Our litanies and our burnt offerings;	*Our prayers and our burnt offerings;*
Therefore no birds trill out a happy note,	*No birds can sing a happy note*
Gorged with the carnival of human gore.	*With their throats stuffed with human gore.*
O ponder this, my son. To err is common	*Think of this, my son. All men*
To all men, but the man who having erred	*Make mistakes, but the man who is mistaken*
Hugs not his errors, but repents and seeks	*Should not hold onto his mistakes, he repents and looks*
The cure, is not a wastrel nor unwise.	*For a cure, if he's not stupid or wasteful.*
No fool, the saw goes, like the obstinate fool.	*There's no fool, the saying goes, like an obstinate fool.*
Let death disarm thy vengeance. O forbear	*Let death calm your vengeance. Do not*
To vex the dead. What glory wilt thou win	*Try to punish the dead. What glory will you win*
By slaying twice the slain? I mean thee well;	*From beating a dead corpse? I mean you well;*
Counsel's most welcome if I promise gain.	*You always liked my advice if it promised good things.*

CREON

Old men, ye all let fly at me your shafts	*Old men, you all fire your arrows at me*
Like archers at a target; yea, ye set	*Like archers at a target; now you set*
Your soothsayer on me. Peddlers are ye all	*Your fortune teller on me. You're all peddlers*
And I the merchandise ye buy and sell.	*And I'm the goods you buy and sell.*
Go to, and make your profit where ye will,	*Get lost, and make your profits elsewhere,*
Silver of Sardis change for gold of Ind;	*Buy Indian gold with Sardinian silver,*
Ye will not purchase this man's burial,	*But you'll never buy this man's burial,*
Not though the winged ministers of Zeus	*Not if the winged messengers of Zeus*
Should bear him in their talons to his throne;	*Carried him up to his throne in their claws;*
Not e'en in awe of prodigy so dire	*Not even my fear of such things*
Would I permit his burial, for I know	*Would make me permit his burial, for I know*
No human soilure can assail the gods;	*No human stain can touch the gods.*

This too I know, Teiresias, dire's the fall

Of craft and cunning when it tries to gloss

Foul treachery with fair words for filthy gain.

I also know this, Teiresias; when skill

And cunning disguise foul treachery

With fair words then it's heading for a nasty fall.

TEIRESIAS

Alas! doth any know and lay to heart--

Alas! Do any know and remember –

CREON

Is this the prelude to some hackneyed saw?

Is this the opening for some clichéd old saying?

TEIRESIAS

How far good counsel is the best of goods?

How much good advice is the best thing of all?

CREON

True, as unwisdom is the worst of ills.

True, as stupidity is the worst thing.

TEIRESIAS

Thou art infected with that ill thyself.

You are infected with that yourself.

CREON

I will not bandy insults with thee, seer.

I won't trade insults with you, fortune teller.

TEIRESIAS

And yet thou say'st my prophesies are frauds.

Yet you say my prophecies are false.

CREON

Prophets are all a money-getting tribe.

Prophets are in it for the profits.

TEIRESIAS

And kings are all a lucre-loving race.

And all kings love money.

CREON

Dost know at whom thou glancest, me thy lord?

Do you know whom you're attacking, me, your lord?

TEIRESIAS

Lord of the State and savior, thanks to me.

Lord and savior of the State – thanks to me.

CREON

Skilled prophet art thou, but to wrong inclined.

You're a skilled prophet, but you lean towards evil.

TEIRESIAS

Take heed, thou wilt provoke me to reveal

Be careful or you'll make me tell

The mystery deep hidden in my breast.

The secret I have hidden deep inside.

CREON

Say on, but see it be not said for gain.

Speak on, but make sure you're not speaking for your profit.

TEIRESIAS

Such thou, methinks, till now hast judged my words.

That's what you think I have been doing up to now.

CREON

Be sure thou wilt not traffic on my wits.

Make sure you don't insult my intelligence.

TEIRESIAS

Know then for sure, the coursers of the sun

Then you should know for sure, that the sun

Not many times shall run their race, before

Will not have risen and set many times before

Thou shalt have given the fruit of thine own loins

You will have given your own child

In quittance of thy murder, life for life;

To pay for the murder you have done, life for life;

For that thou hast entombed a living soul,

For you have buried a living soul,

And sent below a denizen of earth,

And sent a living person to the underworld,

And wronged the nether gods by leaving here

And wronged the gods of that place by leaving

A corpse unlaved, unwept, unsepulchered.

A corpse unwashed, unmourned, unburied.

Herein thou hast no part, nor e'en the gods

You have no say in this, not even the gods

In heaven; and thou usurp'st a power not thine.

Of heaven do; you are assuming a power that's not yours.

For this the avenging spirits of Heaven and Hell

For this the avenging spirits of Heaven and Hell,

Who dog the steps of sin are on thy trail:

What these have suffered thou shalt suffer too.

And now, consider whether bought by gold

I prophesy. For, yet a little while,

And sound of lamentation shall be heard,

Of men and women through thy desolate halls;

And all thy neighbor States are leagues to avenge

Their mangled warriors who have found a grave

I' the maw of wolf or hound, or winged bird

That flying homewards taints their city's air.

These are the shafts, that like a bowman I

Provoked to anger, loosen at thy breast,

Unerring, and their smart thou shalt not shun.

Boy, lead me home, that he may vent his spleen

On younger men, and learn to curb his tongue

With gentler manners than his present mood.

Who chase down sinners, are on your trail:

You shall suffer what you have made others suffer.

And now, think about whether I have been bribed

To say this. For in a little while

The sound of men and women wailing

Shall be heard in your empty halls;

And all your neighboring States will ally to avenge

Their mangled warriors who have found their grave

In the mouth of a wolf or dog, or a bird

That pollutes their city's air as it flies home.

These are the arrows which I, like an archer,

Provoked to anger, fire at your breast,

Well aimed, and you shall not escape their wounds.

Boy, lead me home, leave him to insult

Younger men, and learn to hold his tongue

With better manners than he shows at present.

[Exit **TEIRESIAS**]

CHORUS

My liege, that man hath gone, foretelling woe.

And, O believe me, since these grizzled locks

Were like the raven, never have I known

The prophet's warning to the State to fail.

My lord, the man has gone, predicting sorrow.

And believe me, since these grey hairs

Were jet black, I have never known

The prophet's warning to the State to be wrong.

CREON

I know it too, and it perplexes me.

To yield is grievous, but the obstinate soul

That fights with Fate, is smitten grievously.

CHORUS

Son of Menoeceus, list to good advice.

CREON

What should I do. Advise me. I will heed.

CHORUS

Go, free the maiden from her rocky cell;

And for the unburied outlaw build a tomb.

CREON

Is that your counsel? You would have me yield?

CHORUS

Yea, king, this instant. Vengeance of the gods

Is swift to overtake the impenitent.

CREON

I know that, and it worries me.

To surrender is terrible, but the obstinate soul

Who fights against fate is badly beaten.

Son of Menoeceus, listen to good advice.

What should I do? Advise me, I will listen.

Go, free the girl from her rocky prison,

And build a tomb for the unburied outlaw.

That's your advice? You want me to surrender?

Yes, King, at once. The vengeance of the gods

Soon catches up with the unrepentant.

Ah! what a wrench it is to sacrifice

My heart's resolve; but Fate is ill to fight.

Ah! What a wrench it is to give up

What I'd set my heart on; but it's pointless to fight Fate.

CHORUS

Go, trust not others. Do it quick thyself.

Go, don't trust others; do it yourself.

CREON

I go hot-foot. Bestir ye one and all,

My henchmen! Get ye axes! Speed away

To yonder eminence! I too will go,

For all my resolution this way sways.

'Twas I that bound, I too will set her free.

Almost I am persuaded it is best

To keep through life the law ordained of old.

I'm hurrying there now. Get moving,

Bodyguards! Get axes! Hurry

To that mountain! I'll come too,

For now I'm set on this.

It was I who imprisoned her, I who'll set her free.

I'm almost convinced it's best

Always to stick to the old laws.

[Exit **CREON**]

CHORUS

(Str. 1)

Thou by many names adored,

Child of Zeus the god of thunder,

Of a Theban bride the wonder,

Fair Italia's guardian lord;

In the deep-embosomed glades

You who are worshipped with many names,

Child of Zeus the god of thunder,

Born a miracle from a Theban bride,

The guardian of fair Italy;

In the deep buried places

74

Of the Eleusinian Queen	*Of Persephone,*
Haunt of revelers, men and maids,	*The haunt of revelers, men and women,*
Dionysus, thou art seen.	*You can be seen, Dionysus.*
Where Ismenus rolls his waters,	*Where the river Ismenus flows,*
Where the Dragon's teeth were sown,	*Where the Dragon's teeth were sown,*
Where the Bacchanals thy daughters	*Where you daughters, the Bacchanals,*
Round thee roam,	*Dance around you,*
There thy home;	*That's your home;*
Thebes, O Bacchus, is thine own.	*Thebes, oh Bacchus, belongs to you.*

(Ant. 1)

Thee on the two-crested rock	*We see you on the two crested rock,*
Lurid-flaming torches see;	*With bright flaming torches;*
Where Corisian maidens flock,	*Where the Corsican maidens flock*
Thee the springs of Castaly.	*To you by the springs of Castille.*
By Nysa's bastion ivy-clad,	*By Nysa's ivy-clad castle,*
By shores with clustered vineyards glad,	*By the shores with their happy vineyards,*
There to thee the hymn rings out,	*There the hymn is sung to you,*
And through our streets we Thebans shout,	*And in the streets we Thebans shout,*
All hail to thee	*All praise to you,*
Evoe, Evoe!	*Hail, hail!*

(Str. 2)

Oh, as thou lov'st this city best of all,	*As you love this city most of all,*
To thee, and to thy Mother levin-stricken,	*To you, and your lightning-struck mother,*
In our dire need we call;	*We call out in our great need;*

Thou see'st with what a plague our townsfolk sicken.

Thy ready help we crave,

Whether adown Parnassian heights descending,

Or o'er the roaring straits thy swift was wending,

Save us, O save!

You see what an illness strikes our townsfolk.

We crave your help,

Whether you come down from Parnassus,

Or come flying over the roaring sea,

Save us, save us!

(Ant. 2)

Brightest of all the orbs that breathe forth light,

Authentic son of Zeus, immortal king,

Leader of all the voices of the night,

Come, and thy train of Thyiads with thee bring,

Thy maddened rout

Who dance before thee all night long, and shout,

Thy handmaids we,

Evoe, Evoe!

Brightest of all the stars,

Real son of Zeus, the immortal King,

Leader of all the voices of the night,

Come, and bring your Bacchantes with you,

Your frenzied followers,

Who dance before you all night long, and shout,

We are your handmaids,

Hail, hail!

[Enter **MESSENGER**]

MESSENGER

Attend all ye who dwell beside the halls

Of Cadmus and Amphion. No man's life

As of one tenor would I praise or blame,

For Fortune with a constant ebb and rise

Casts down and raises high and low alike,

And none can read a mortal's horoscope.

Take Creon; he, methought, if any man,

Listen all who live in the lands

Of Cadmus and Amphion. No man's life

Can be said to be just good or bad,

For fate ebbs and flows and

Throws down and elevates high and low alike,

And no man can tell the future.

Take Creon; he, I thought, of all men

Was enviable. He had saved this land
Of Cadmus from our enemies and attained
A monarch's powers and ruled the state supreme,
While a right noble issue crowned his bliss.
Now all is gone and wasted, for a life
Without life's joys I count a living death.
You'll tell me he has ample store of wealth,
The pomp and circumstance of kings; but if
These give no pleasure, all the rest I count
The shadow of a shade, nor would I weigh
His wealth and power 'gainst a dram of joy.

Was to be envied. He saved this land
Of Cadmus from our enemies, gained
A king's powers and ruled the State alone,
And he had a noble son to seal his happiness.
Now it is all gone and ruined, for a life
Without life's pleasures I call a living death.
You'll tell me he has plenty of money,
And all the trappings that go with being a king; but if
These give no pleasure, I rate all the rest
As a ghostly shadow, nor would I exchange
His wealth and power for one drop of joy.

CHORUS

What fresh woes bring'st thou to the royal house?

What fresh sorrow do you bring to the royal house?

MESSENGER

Both dead, and they who live deserve to die.

They're both dead, and there are those alive who
deserve death.

CHORUS

Who is the slayer, who the victim? speak.

Who is the killer, who's the victim? Speak.

MESSENGER

Haemon; his blood shed by no stranger hand.

Haemon, and his blood was not shed by a stranger's

hand.

CHORUS

What mean ye? by his father's or his own?

What do you mean? By his father's or his own?

MESSENGER

His own; in anger for his father's crime.

His own, in protest at his father's crime.

CHORUS

O prophet, what thou spakest comes to pass.

Oh prophet, what you predicted has happened.

MESSENGER

So stands the case; now 'tis for you to act.

That's the situation; now you must act.

CHORUS

Lo! from the palace gates I see approaching

Creon's unhappy wife, Eurydice.

Comes she by chance or learning her son's fate?

Look! From the palace gates I see coming

Creon's unhappy wife, Eurydice.

Has she come by chance or does she know her son's

fate?

[Enter **EURYDICE**]

EURYDICE

Ye men of Thebes, I overheard your talk.

As I passed out to offer up my prayer

To Pallas, and was drawing back the bar

To open wide the door, upon my ears

There broke a wail that told of household woe

Stricken with terror in my handmaids' arms

I fell and fainted. But repeat your tale

To one not unacquaint with misery.

You men of Thebes, I overheard your talk.

As I was going out to make my prayers

To Pallas, and was drawing back the bolts

To throw open the door, on my ears

There crashed a wail that told of a tragedy for the household;

Struck down by terror I fell and fainted

In my handmaid's arms. But repeat your tale

To one who is used to misery.

MESSENGER

Dear mistress, I was there and will relate

The perfect truth, omitting not one word.

Why should we gloze and flatter, to be proved

Liars hereafter? Truth is ever best.

Well, in attendance on my liege, your lord,

I crossed the plain to its utmost margin, where

The corse of Polyneices, gnawn and mauled,

Was lying yet. We offered first a prayer

To Pluto and the goddess of cross-ways,

With contrite hearts, to deprecate their ire.

Then laved with lustral waves the mangled corse,

Laid it on fresh-lopped branches, lit a pyre,

And to his memory piled a mighty mound

Of mother earth. Then to the caverned rock,

The bridal chamber of the maid and Death,

Dear mistress, I was there and will tell

The absolute truth, omitting nothing.

Why should we disguise and flatter, to be shown

As liars afterwards? The truth is always best.

Well, in attendance on my master, your lord,

I crossed to the farthest edge of the plain, where

The corpse of Polynieces, chewed and mauled,

Was still lying. We offered up a prayer

To Pluto and the goddess of crossroads,

With humble hearts, to soften their anger.

Then we washed the mangled corpse with purifying streams,

Put fresh-cut branches on it, lit a pyre,

And in his memory piled up a great

Earth mound. Then we went to the rocky cave,

The place the girl was to married with Death,

We sped, about to enter. But a guard	*As quickly as we could, and were about to enter. But a guard*
Heard from that godless shrine a far shrill wail,	*Heard from that godless place a far off scream,*
And ran back to our lord to tell the news.	*And ran back to tell our lord the news.*
But as he nearer drew a hollow sound	*But as he got nearer the hollow moans*
Of lamentation to the King was borne.	*Of mourning reached the King.*
He groaned and uttered then this bitter plaint:	*He groaned and said these bitter words:*
"Am I a prophet? miserable me!	*"Am I a prophet? Oh misery!*
Is this the saddest path I ever trod?	*Is this the saddest road I ever took?*
'Tis my son's voice that calls me. On press on,	*That's my son's voice. Hurry on,*
My henchmen, haste with double speed to the tomb	*Guards, as fast as you can to the tomb*
Where rocks down-torn have made a gap, look in	*Where rocks have been torn down to make a gap, look in*
And tell me if in truth I recognize	*And tell me if I am right to think that was*
The voice of Haemon or am heaven-deceived."	*The voice of Haemon, or am I tricked by heaven?"*
So at the bidding of our distraught lord	*So at the orders or our distraught lord*
We looked, and in the craven's vaulted gloom	*We looked, and in the cavern's gloom*
I saw the maiden lying strangled there,	*I saw the girl lying there strangled*
A noose of linen twined about her neck;	*With a linen noose around her neck;*
And hard beside her, clasping her cold form,	*Right next to her, holding her cold body,*
Her lover lay bewailing his dead bride	*Was her lover, mourning his dead bride*
Death-wedded, and his father's cruelty.	*Who had married death, and cursing his father's cruelty.*
When the King saw him, with a terrible groan	*When the King saw him, with a terrible groan*
He moved towards him, crying, "O my son	*He went towards him, crying, "Oh my son,*
What hast thou done? What ailed thee? What mischance	*What have you done? What troubled you? What mishap*
Has reft thee of thy reason? O come forth,	*Has made you mad? Oh come outside,*
Come forth, my son; thy father supplicates."	*Come out, my son, your father begs you."*
But the son glared at him with tiger eyes,	*But the son glared at him with fierce eyes,*

Spat in his face, and then, without a word,

Drew his two-hilted sword and smote, but missed

His father flying backwards. Then the boy,

Wroth with himself, poor wretch, incontinent

Fell on his sword and drove it through his side

Home, but yet breathing clasped in his lax arms

The maid, her pallid cheek incarnadined

With his expiring gasps. So there they lay

Two corpses, one in death. His marriage rites

Are consummated in the halls of Death:

A witness that of ills whate'er befall

Mortals' unwisdom is the worst of all.

Spat on his face and then, without a word,

Drew his two handed sword and struck, but missed,

His father flew backwards. Then the boy,

Furious with himself, poor wretch, uncontrollably

Fell on his sword and drove it through his side,

Then still breathing he held the girl in his

Weak arms, her white cheek reddened

With his dying breaths. So there they lay,

Two corpses, together in death. His marriage ceremony

Will be performed in the underworld;

It shows that of all the evils in the world,

Men's stupidity is the worst.

[Exit **EURYDICE**]

CHORUS

What makest thou of this? The Queen has gone

Without a word importing good or ill.

What do you make of this? The Queen has gone

Without saying a word, good or bad.

MESSENGER

I marvel too, but entertain good hope.

'Tis that she shrinks in public to lament

Her son's sad ending, and in privacy

Would with her maidens mourn a private loss.

Trust me, she is discreet and will not err.

I'm surprised too, but don't be afraid.

I'm sure she doesn't want to mourn her son's sad death

In public, and wants to mourn her private loss

In privacy with her handmaidens.

Trust me, she is careful and won't do anything wrong.

CHORUS

I know not, but strained silence, so I deem,

Is no less ominous than excessive grief.

I don't know – I think strained silence

Can be a worse sign than excessive grief.

MESSENGER

Well, let us to the house and solve our doubts,

Whether the tumult of her heart conceals

Some fell design. It may be thou art right:

Unnatural silence signifies no good.

Well, let's go inside and find out

Whether the storm in her heart has hidden

Some evil plan. It may be that you're right;

Unnatural silence is not good.

CHORUS

Lo! the King himself appears.

Evidence he with him bears

'Gainst himself (ah me! I quake

'Gainst a king such charge to make)

But all must own,

The guilt is his and his alone.

Look! The King himself is here.

He is carrying evidence of his guilt;

I fear to lay charges against a king,

But everyone must admit

That his guilt is his and his alone.

CREON

Woe for sin of minds perverse,

Deadly fraught with mortal curse.

Behold us slain and slayers, all akin.

Woe for my counsel dire, conceived in sin.

    Alas, my son,

Alas for the sin of twisted minds,

Fatally wounded with a mortal curse.

Look at us, killed and killers, all alike.

Alas for my dreadful ideas, born of sin.

Alas, my son,

Life scarce begun,

Thou wast undone.

The fault was mine, mine only, O my son!

Your life had hardly begun,

And now it's over.

It was my fault, only my fault, my son!

CHORUS

Too late thou seemest to perceive the truth.

It seems you've seen the truth too late.

CREON

By sorrow schooled. Heavy the hand of god,

I have learnt through sadness. The punishment of god is heavy,

Thorny and rough the paths my feet have trod,

Humbled my pride, my pleasure turned to pain;

Poor mortals, how we labor all in vain!

My feet have trodden thorny rough paths,

My pride is humbled and my pleasure turned to pain;

Poor mortals, how we slave away for nothing.

[Enter **SECOND MESSENGER**]

SECOND MESSENGER

Sorrows are thine, my lord, and more to come,

One lying at thy feet, another yet

More grievous waits thee, when thou comest home.

You have sorrows, my lord, and there are more to come.

There is one lying at your feet, and a worse one

Awaits you when you come home.

CREON

What woe is lacking to my tale of woes?

How can there be any more sadness for me?

SECOND MESSENGER

Thy wife, the mother of thy dead son here,

Lies stricken by a fresh inflicted blow.

Your wife, the mother of your dead son here,

Lies struck down by a recent blow.

CREON

How bottomless the pit!

Does claim me too, O Death?

What is this word he saith,

This woeful messenger? Say, is it fit

To slay anew a man already slain?

Is Death at work again,

Stroke upon stroke, first son, then mother slain?

How deep the pit is!

Do you want me too, oh Death?

What does he say,

This sad messenger? Is it right

To kill a man a second time?

Is Death at work again,

Blow after blow, first the son and now the mother dead?

CHORUS

Look for thyself. She lies for all to view.

Look for yourself. There she is for all to see.

CREON

Alas! another added woe I see.

What more remains to crown my agony?

A minute past I clasped a lifeless son,

And now another victim Death hath won.

Unhappy mother, most unhappy son!

Alas! I see another sorrow.

What's left to add to my pain?

A minute ago I held a lifeless son,

And now Death has taken another victim.

Unhappy mother, most unhappy son!

SECOND MESSENGER

Beside the altar on a keen-edged sword

She fell and closed her eyes in night, but erst

She mourned for Megareus who nobly died

Long since, then for her son; with her last breath

She cursed thee, the slayer of her child.

Beside the altar she fell on a keen edged sword

And closed her eyes in darkness, but first

She mourned for Megareus who nobly died

Long ago, then she mourned her son; with her last breath

She cursed you, the slayer of her child.

CREON

I shudder with affright

O for a two-edged sword to slay outright

A wretch like me,

Made one with misery.

I shudder with fear.

Oh for a sharp sword to kill

A wretch like me,

Who is as one with misery.

SECOND MESSENGER

'Tis true that thou wert charged by the dead Queen

As author of both deaths, hers and her son's.

It's true that you were accused by the dead Queen

Of being guilty of both deaths, hers and her son's.

CREON

In what wise was her self-destruction wrought?

In what way did she kill herself?

SECOND MESSENGER

Hearing the loud lament above her son

Hearing the loud mourning over her son

With her own hand she stabbed herself to the heart.　*She stabbed herself through the heart.*

CREON

I am the guilty cause. I did the deed,　*I am the guilty one.　I did the deed,*

Thy murderer. Yea, I guilty plead.　*I'm the murderer.　Yes, I plead guilty.*

My henchmen, lead me hence, away, away,　*Guards, take me away, away, away!*

A cipher, less than nothing; no delay!　*I have no worth, I'm less than nothing; don't wait!*

CHORUS

Well said, if in disaster aught is well　*It's true that if anything good comes from disaster*

His past endure demand the speediest cure.　*It's that the suffering calls for the swiftest cure.*

CREON

Come, Fate, a friend at need,　*Come, friend, I need you now,*

Come with all speed!　*Hurry!*

Come, my best friend,　*Come, my best friend,*

And speed my end!　*Finish me!*

Away, away!　*Come on!*

Let me not look upon another day!　*Don't let me see another day!*

CHORUS

This for the morrow; to us are present needs　*This is for tomorrow; at the moment there are pressing matters*

That they whom it concerns must take in hand.　*Which those whom they concern must deal with.*

86

CREON

I join your prayer that echoes my desire.

I join in your prayer which echoes my wishes.

CHORUS

O pray not, prayers are idle; from the doom

Of fate for mortals refuge is there none.

Oh don't pray, prayers are useless; from the fate

Of Death there is no hiding place.

CREON

Away with me, a worthless wretch who slew

Unwitting thee, my son, thy mother too.

Whither to turn I know not; every way

Leads but astray,

And on my head I feel the heavy weight

Of crushing Fate.

Take me away, a worthless wretch who killed,

Not meaning to, you, my son, and your mother too.

I don't know which way to turn; every way

Just leads to wrong,

And on my head I can feel the heavy weight

Of crushing fate.

CHORUS

Of happiness the chiefest part

Is a wise heart:

And to defraud the gods in aught

With peril's fraught.

Swelling words of high-flown might

Mightily the gods do smite.

Chastisement for errors past

Wisdom brings to age at last.

The thing that's needed most for happiness

Is a wise heart:

To cheat the gods in anything

Is full of danger.

Great words, full of pride,

Are struck down mightily by the gods.

Punishment for past sins

Brings wisdom to age in the end.

47567867R00050

Made in the USA
Columbia, SC
02 January 2019